Vincentia Schroeter, Margit Koemeda-Lutz, Maê Nascimento (Eds.)
Bioenergetic Analysis 2016 (26)

edition psychosozial

Vincentia Schroeter, Margit Koemeda-Lutz,
Maê Nascimento (Eds.)

Bioenergetic Analysis

The Clinical Journal of the
International Institute for Bioenergetic Analysis
(2016) Volume 26

Psychosozial-Verlag

Submissions for consideration for the next volume of *Bioenergetic Analysis* must be sent to the editor (vincentiaschroeter@gmail.com) between June 1st and September 1st, 2016.

Bibliographic information of Die Deutsche Nationalbibliothek (The German Library)
The Deutsche Nationalbibliothek lists this publication in the
Deutsche Nationalbibliografie; detailed bibliographic data
are available at http://dnb.d-nb.de.

Original edition

info@psychosozial-verlag.de
www.psychosozial-verlag.de

Cover: Sabine Strenger-Rehberger: o.T., 1997
Cover design & layout based on drafts by Hanspeter Ludwig, Wetzlar
www.imaginary-world.de
ISBN 978-3-8379-2504-3

Content

Reviewers for this issue were:
Tarra Stariell
Bob Lewis
Scott Baum
Joerg Clauer
Angela Klopstech
Odila Weigand

Letter from the Editor

This was a year when more valid papers were received for consideration than could be accommodated. I think this shows an energetic excitement in sharing newfound ideas and concepts. The Bioenergetic community is investigating new material, including exciting scientific research linking the body and the brain. Clinicians not trained in any type of somatic psychotherapy cannot ignore the links to the body touted in all the latest research. In larger numbers they are looking to incorporate somatic psychotherapy theory and techniques into their thinking. They are seeking out trainings and readings to translate this material into their current practices. Bioenergetics, founded on psychoanalysis, body-based as per the theories of Lowen, and now modernized with neuroscience can help them. This volume can also help the Bioenergetic clinician. For example, Bioenergetic Analysts are weaving polyvagal theory into their thinking, clinical work and writing. In this volume alone, Heinrich-Clauer, Schroeter and Clauer all refer to polyvagal theory in their papers.

In addition, Perlman writes about defenses and openings around falling, holding and grounding. We have a paper of evidence-based research examining treatment effectiveness for different types of therapy by Koemeda. A personal essay, with a poetic flair, which is on finding the ground of home by Conger, breaks up the more theoretical papers.

I thank these authors for their contribution as well as my editing team, Mae Nascimento, and Margit Koemeda for all their help and support. Readers and reviewers include Tarra Stariell, Bob Lewis, Scott Baum, Joerg Clauer, Angela Klopstech, and Odila Weigand. I send thanks to the translators of abstracts, Guy Tonella, Louise Frechette, Violaine de Clerk, Sylvia Nunez, Mae Nascimento, and Margit Koemeda. This entire volume will be translated into Italian by Maria Rosaria Filoni.

In closing I would like to share in this letter some inspiring and thoughtful words taken from President Garry Cockburn's opening address at the well-attended and well-received IIBA conference in Brazil, Summer of 2015:

> "In contrast to the neurotic and rigid personality structures of Reich and Lowen's world, today, people's psyches are too exposed and in danger of fragmenting in the face of the social forces and global threats I mentioned. So what is needed is not a strong therapy that breaks people open. We are already too open.
>
> What we need is a strong therapy that allows us to have the courage to be where there is little or no structure, where we risk knowing the terrors of traumatic abandonment, fragmentation and annihilation, but … where we know and trust that there is a somatic reality even in those depths that is capable of being redeemed by the touch of another. We cannot exist at those depths without the other, otherwise we risk psychosis or autistic encapsulation. And we cannot save this earth without needing and loving each other with a passion. We are all brothers and sisters on this earth, and more than ever, we need to love our neighbour, no matter what their creed, gender preference, colour or politics.
>
> We have to deepen our understanding of what we have inherited from Lowen in order to meet this challenge. We have to articulate a more complex formulation of Bioenergetic Analysis in the world today, while maintaining the substance of what Lowen has given us about the bodily self. We need to more deeply understand how to do body therapy at this primitive level and at the level of early relational trauma, and to trust that the face and body of another is deeply programmed into our DNA …
>
> What Bioenergetic Analysis gives us is the unifying focus and power of Lowen's insight: that freeing the human body from unconscious terror and fear is the key to restoring the powerful loving relationship with ourselves, with each other, with nature and with the environment."

Welcome to the 26th volume of Bioenergetic Analysis. May you enjoy these papers and may they be a forum to do for you what Garry advocates above, "articulate a more complex formulation of Bioenergetic Analysis in the world today."

Vincentia Schroeter, PhD
San Marcos, Ca. USA
October 31st, 2015

Polyvagal Theory

Introduction for Somatic Psychotherapy

Vincentia Schroeter

Abstracts

English

This paper introduces polyvagal theory (1995) as defined by its originator, Stephen Porges, for the benefit of somatic, body-oriented, clinical psychotherapists. While there has been a recent explosion of interest in integrating this psychophysiological theory within various fields, some of the references to and explanation of the material can be difficult to grasp. The goal of this paper is to provide a clear explication of this theory. The main tenets of polyvagal theory will be presented including neuroception, the old and new view of the autonomic nervous system (ANS), normal and stress functions of the ANS, and trauma and attachment from a polyvagal point of view. Case material will illustrate somatic relational techniques from an ANS lens. The use of anatomical portals to contact or promote shifts will be provided.

Key words: polyvagal, neuroception, autonomic nervous system, sympathetic, social engagement system, vagal brake, portals

German

Dieser Beitrag gibt für somatische, körper-orientierte und klinische Psychotherapeut/innen eine Einführung in die Polyvagal-Theorie, wie sie von ihrem Begründer Stephen Porges entwickelt wurde. Während in jüngster Zeit ein explodierendes Interesse an der Integration dieser psychophysiologischen Theorie auf verschiedenen Gebieten zu verzeichnen war, sind einige Hinweise auf und Erklärungen zu dem betreffenden Material schwer zu verstehen. Ziel dieses Beitrags ist es, eine klare Darstellung der Theorie zu liefern. Es werden die hauptsächlichen Konzeptualisierungen der Polyvagal-Theorie vorgetragen, einschließlich der Neurozeption, der alten und einer neuen Sichtweise des Autonomen Nervensystems (ANS), normale und Stress-bedingte Funktionsweisen des ANS, Trauma und Bindung aus einer polyvagalen Perspektive. Fallbeispiele illustrieren beziehungsorientierte, körperpsychotherapeutische Techniken aus einem ANS-bezogenen Blickwinkel. Die Nutzung anatomischer Portale, um Veränderung wahrzunehmen oder zu initiieren, wird erläutert.

French

Cet article présente la théorie polyvagale telle que son concepteur, Stephen Porges (1995), l'a définie, constituant un apport majeur pour les psychothérapeutes, qu'ils soient d'orientation psychosomatique ou psychocorporelle. Il existe aujourd'hui un extraordinaire intérêt à intégrer cette théorie psychophysiologique dans ces divers champs, mais quelques unes de ses références ou de ses explications peuvent rester difficiles à saisir. L'objectif de cet article est d'en proposer une vision claire. Les grands principes de la théorie polyvagale y seront présentés, incluant la neuroception, l'ancienne et la nouvelle appréhension du système nerveux autonome (SNA), les fonctions du SNA normales et relatives au stress, une vision du trauma et de l'attachement du point de vue polyvagal. Des cas cliniques illustreront des techniques somatiques-relationnelles passées par le filtre du SNA. L'utilisation de portails anatomiques sera proposée afin de promouvoir le changement.

Spanish

Este ensayo introduce la teoría polivagal (1995) tal y como la define su creador, Stephen Porges, para el beneficio de los psicoterapeutas clínicos de orientación somática del cuerpo. Aunque ha habido una reciente explosión de interés en la integración de esta teoría psicofisiológica en diversos ámbitos, algunas de las referencias sobre la explicación del material pueden ser difíciles de entender. El objetivo de este ensayo es el de proporcionar una aclaración acerca de esta teoría. Se presentarán los postulados principales de la teoría polivagal, incluyendo la neurocepción, las consideraciones antiguas y nuevas sobre el sistema nervioso autónomo (SNA), las funciones normales y estresadas del SNA, y el tema del trauma y el apego desde un punto de vista polivagal. El material de los casos prácticos ilustrará las técnicas relacionales somáticas a través de las lentes del SNA. Se proporcionará el uso de portales anatómicos para contactar o promover cambios.

Portuguese

Este artigo apresenta a Teoria Polivagal (1995), tal como é definida por seu fundador, Stephen Porges, no intuito de auxiliar psicoterapeutas que seguem orientações clínicas somáticas e corporais. Embora haja uma recente explosão de interesse em integrar esta teoria psicofisiológica com diversos campos, algumas referências e explicações desse material podem ser de difícil entendimento. O objetivo deste artigo é fornecer uma explicação clara desta teoria. Serão apresentados, aqui, os princípios fundamentais da Teoria Polivagal, incluindo neurocepção, a antiga e a nova visão do Sistema Nervoso Autônomo (SNA), funções normal e de stress do SNA e trauma e apego a partir do ponto de vista polivagal. Material de estudos de caso ilustram técnicas somático-relacionais através da lente do SNA, assim como se demonstra o uso de portais anatômicos relativos ao contato ou à promoção de mudanças.

I. Introduction

Interest in polyvagal theory has been spreading as it lends a valuable new view of human behavior from a neurological point of view. Within psychology, polyvagal theory has broad clinical applications and has influenced the understanding and treatment of many issues including trauma, personality disorders, and childhood challenges, such as autism. While many psychotherapists are integrating Polyvagal Theory into their clinical understanding and practice (including articles in this journal: see Heinrich-Clauer (2016), Shahri (2014, 2017), Clauer (2016), also Clauer workshop, IIBA conference (2011), the theoretical information can appear complex, particularly due to the dense writing of the book introducing polyvagal theory by it's originator, Stephen Porges. The book, *The Polyvagal Theory: Neurophysiological Foundations of Emotions, Attachment, Communication, Self-Regulation* is available in English, German (published in 2010) and is currently being translated into Italian.

Since its publication (2011), Porges has become a sought after and clearer communicator as interest in his research has exploded into and benefited many fields, such as neurology, medicine, biology, education, psychology, communication, and mindfulness. Others (notably John Chitty) have interpreted his work for psychology in an easier to grasp fashion. Some of Chitty's visual material (used by permission) will be included in this paper. This paper proposes to add to the clarification of terms and concepts for the benefit of psychotherapists who wish to become more familiar with polyvagal theory and to apply it to the clinical setting.

A. Bioenergetics and the Historical Centrality of the Body

Bioenergetics as developed by Alexander Lowen (1957) has always placed the body, along with its arousal and regulation at the center of therapeutic action. Lowen's predecessor, Wilhelm Reich (1930), observed that the body responds automatically and defensively to states of emotional arousal, painful or pleasurable, and that the body and its patterns of armoring should therefore be central in psychoanalytic inquiry and intervention. The unity of psyche and soma with the soma (body) as the main target of intervention was rejected by Freud and most of his followers. Reich observed and defined various body-types as responses in characteristic patterns of tension (character types), which arise from developmental wounding. While Reich's theoretical ideas were lauded and studied in psychoanalytic circles for many years (*Character Analysis*, 1933), the bridge from theory to working somatically as the central technique to healing was never widely accepted. So Reich created his own school (The School of Social Research) to teach his method, and Bioenergetics was the next generation of his work.

Other somatic psychotherapies focusing on the body sprang up over the years, such as Feldenkrais, Hellerwork, and Radix, but none with the same strong ties to psychoanalytic understanding as Bioenergetics. The developmentally adaptive organism as manifest in the physical body, (even with application of modern shifts in psychodynamic theory), has always been at the main center of therapeutic focus in Bioenergetics. The emphasis is on mobilizing the organism away from defensive and toward healthy emotional and affective processes as they are seen in the body.

While the emphasis has been to mobilize the organism away from defensive, destructive processes and toward emotionally healthy processes, it is polyvagal theory that sheds a light on the inner workings of the nervous system in a way that helps us understand more deeply the mechanisms of defense and healthy emotional communication on a body level. Following a short introduction to Porges, parts of an interview will be presented. In the interview Porges supports the somatically oriented psychotherapist as the only clinician who does not just work "top-down" (from head to body only) and who understands the bi-directional communication of body and brain that he (Porges) has now scientifically backed up by his theory.

B. Introduction to Stephen Porges' Theory

1. *Background*

Stephen W. Porges is a neuroscientist interested in the neurobiology of human behavior. He is a university scientist at the Kinsey Institute at Indiana University and research professor of psychiatry in North Carolina, USA. Polyvagal Theory (hereafter referred to as PT) is a contribution to psychophysiology, which crosses many disciplines and is particularly relevant for somatic psychotherapy. Integrative studies linking the central nervous system (CNS) to autonomic function, such as PT (Porges, 1995, 2003) are new. Porges coined the term, "polyvagal" to emphasize three rather than the traditionally understood two branches of the ANS (Porges, 1995).

PT introduces a new perspective that:

a. Relates autonomic function to behavior that sees the autonomic nervous system (ANS) as a "system."
b. Identifies neural circuits involved in regulating autonomic states.
c. Interprets autonomic reactivity as adaptive from a phylogenetic perspective.

Porges created a groundbreaking contribution to our understanding of the human organism in terms of how our nervous system functions and how it regulates our visceral system. As part of the explosion of research in neuroscience, he has provided new links and confirmed heretofore mystical connections between the brain, the organs and affective parts of the body. For instance, they really do communicate back and forth! The bi-directional communication of organs to brain, as well as brain to body is revolutionary. PT also adds to our understanding of the reactivity of humans, particularly under stress. Since publishing his seminal book (2011), Porges has continued his mission to do scientific research and to communicate his new understanding of the ANS (Automatic Nervous System) as it applies to many fields. His own website www.stephenporges.com has many articles, interviews and videos.

Although his book can be dense and repetitive, it contains valuable physiological detail that will not be included in this paper. Next, are some notes from an interview with Porges where he supports the somatic psychotherapy world as respecting the bi-directional travels of brain and body communication.

2. *The Nervous System and Visceral Feelings*

Here are some notes from Serge Prengel's interview of Porges (www.somaticperspectives.com):

Serge Prengel: How does our nervous system interplay with our visceral feelings?
Stephen Porges: Although the important role that the nervous system plays in regulating our visceral state and thus our feelings is a relevant question for people interested in body psychotherapy, it is not even acknowledged in many of the models, theories, and therapies emphasized in clinical psychology and psychiatry. Clinical psychology and psychiatry primarily use top-down models that focus on emotions and affective processes as being central phenomena and minimize the role of the body in the experience. For example, consistent with these models, even anxiety may be a "brain" process without a visceral manifestation. Fortunately, there are clinicians, including many body psychotherapists, who have an appreciation of the importance of the bidirectional communication between the brain and the body. For example, sensory information travels from the body to the brain and influences how we respond to the world. And brain processes can influence our viscera via the cognitive and affective processes related to our perspective of the world and our reactions to various features of the environment. This bidirectional and interactive notion of how our nervous system regulates our viscera in a complex social environment, although intuitive, is neglected or minimized by much of clinical medicine including psychiatry.

So Porges is acknowledging body psychotherapy at the forefront of the movement to incorporate this "bidirectional" communication between body and brain. In his book he writes about the *efferent* (from brain down) and *afferent* (from the organs up to the head) communication that exists. The neglect he speaks of is changing in many circles, as we digest and incorporate this valuable knowledge from polyvagal theory. The main concepts of this theory are covered next.

3. Triune Brain

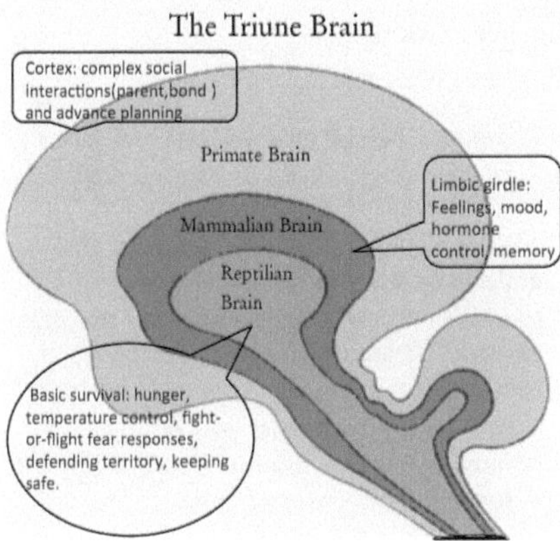

Figure 1. The Triune Brain

The triune brain is made up of the brainstem, which houses the most primitive reptilian brain; the limbic, shared with other mammals; and the neo-cortex, that primates have and is most developed in humans.

II. Main Concepts: Polyvagal Theory

A. Neuroception

1. Introduction to Neuroception

This term was coined by Porges to define an automatic process. Neuroception is an unconscious detection of safety or danger. For example, when we are in nature, we may see what looks like a snake on the road. We immediately freeze in an alert state. We do not go closer until we assess that it is just a stick and not a dangerous snake. The automaticity of the response is evolutionarily adaptive for when quick action is needed to survive danger. The "survival of the fittest" was a term coined by Spencer (1864). In groups this survival depended on both trust and bonding with others and also this neuroception of danger. If the tiger is heard or an enemy tribe spotted, instant reaction could be the difference between life and death. Our ancestors who wanted to think too long before acting in crisis situations like life threat, probably died. Those that lived on, these survivors, carried neuroception prowess to succeeding generations.

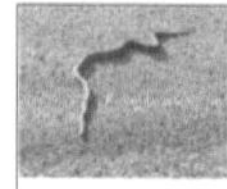

Neuroception

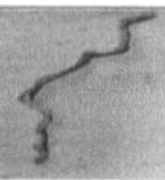

- A subconscious system for detecting threats and safety at a glance.
- Neural circuits distinguish whether situations are safe, dangerous, or life threatening.
- IS THAT A SNAKE OR A STICK IN THE ROAD?
- Faulty neuroception: inability to inhibit defense in safe environment and/or activate defense in risky environment.

Figure 2. Neuroception Chart

2. *Neuroception: Application to Psychotherapy*

Neuroception is the unconscious assessment of safety versus danger that is part of the ANS. Understanding this instinct helps the client as well as the therapist feel compassion for choices that are made. Every choice can be seen through the useful lens of safety (perceived or real) versus danger (perceived or real). *Faulty neuroception* occurs when a person misperceives safety or danger. For instance, a person who lives in a generally safe neighborhood is afraid to walk outside their front door for fear of being accosted. This person sees danger where objectively there is none. On the other hand, feeling safe in a dangerous environment is also faulty neuroception. For example, walking down a dark alley in a carefree manner in a seedy neighborhood at night indicates a poor ability to *neurocept* or discern danger, where it exists.

3. *Clinical Vignette Illustrating Neuroception*

The following is provided to show an example of neuroception.

A female client who I have been seeing for years comes into her weekly session feeling happy, in a much better mood than last week, when she was depressed and not wanting to go for walks alone in her safe neighborhood. She did not want to venture out alone, even though she knew the exercise had potential to lift her depression. The reason was that she would see other happy couples and families on her walk. She was fearful the walk would provoke sadness at her recent relationship breakup. This caused her to contract, pull in toward herself and not take her walk outside. This pulling in is *instinctive* and feels protective due to the *perceived danger* of feeling the unwanted emotion of sadness. Her neuroception told her it was dangerous to go for a walk alone.

Perceived danger relates to a past trauma in her case. Dipping into sadness scares her because of her history. When her mother was dying she stopped eating, became catatonic, suffered severe depression, had a psychotic break and had to be hospitalized for an extended time. Although stable for many years, opening sadness triggers her fear of another psychotic break. Therefore, her avoiding the walk was a protection against a danger of decompensation.

B. ANS Old View versus New View

1. Introduction to New versus Old ANS View

Porges' work changes what we learned about the autonomic nervous system from a dual antagonistic system (with two levels of response) to a hierarchical system with three levels of response to stimuli. The old view, the dual antagonistic system believed we go back and forth, like on a seesaw from hyperarousal (danger but not life threatening) to hypoarousal (life threat). The new view includes the important extra and evolutionarily newest branch, known as the SES (social engagement system). The three branches have different functions under normal conditions and under stress. The charts (used by permission) below were created by John Chitty (chapter 6, *Dancing with Yin and Yang*) and are clear illustrations of these three levels and their functions. According to Jackson's theory of dissolution (see fig. 5), we use our phylogenetically newest system (SES) first UNDER STRESS, if it fails we use the next (SNS), if that fails we go to the most primitive system (PNS).

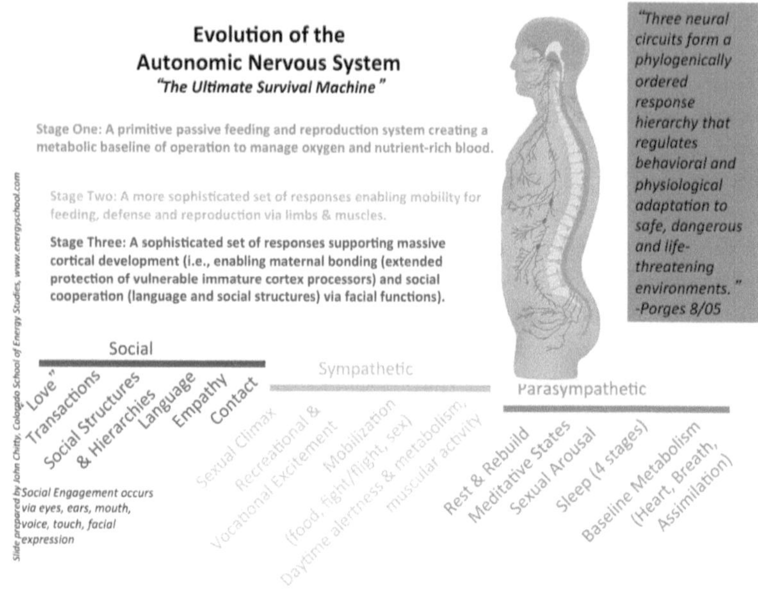

Figure 3. ANS 1

2. *Normal Functions of ANS*

The chart (see fig. 3: ANS 1) shows the normal functions of the three parts of the ANS. The ANS evolved in three stages over time. Stage one, is the oldest phylogenetically and most primitive. We share this system, the *parasympathetic*, with reptiles. This has been referred to as, "the lizard brain." Stage two, the *sympathetic*, occurs in animals further up the food chain, including mammals. This has been referred to as, "the mouse brain." The most sophisticated system, stage three, is most highly developed in humans. This is the "new" area examined and highlighted by Porges in a way that has changed our thinking about the workings of the ANS.

3. *Bonding Phylogeny*

To illustrate all three levels, bonding with offspring will be used. Reptiles do not bond with their offspring. Once they are born babies instinctively move out into the world on their own. Animals, including birds and mammals, have a longer period of dependency on parents once they are born. Animals take care of their young by providing warmth, protection and feeding until the offspring can fend for themselves. The most recently formed is the *social engagement system* (aka "the communication system"). Although other mammals have some bonding and communication capacities like humans, this system is more developed in primates and is most developed in humans. Our young are dependent on caretaking longer than other animals, and therefore parents need sophisticated skills to keep them safe and babies need sophisticated skills to communicate their needs. We use our eyes, ears, voice, touch and facial expressions to maximize proximity for safety and bonding.

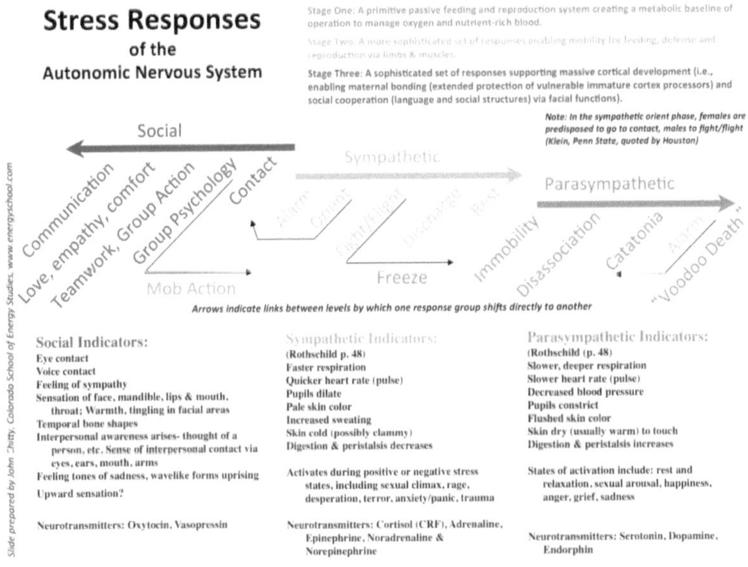

Figure 4. ANS 2

4. *Stress Functions of the ANS*

Figure 4: ANS 2 shows the stress response of the ANS. This is a crucial contribution to deepening our understanding of how the ANS operates in humans. The links show shifts from one system directly to another. For example, while the SES is usually a positive, calm yet engaged zone, where one feels safe and not under threat, notice that a strong identification with a group can cause a group psychology that solidifies into an "us against them" mentality that can make the group feel threatened, which can lead to a mob action. This automatically shifts the person into the SNS, ready to fight for the cause. An example might be a fundamental religious group that preaches tolerance, but feels so threatened by "non-believers" that they enter into a combative relationship with one group or another.

5. *CAUTION: In Viewing Normal versus Stress ANS Figures*

These charts (fig. 3: ANS 1 and fig. 4: ANS 2) show the normal and stress response of each level. It is important not to mix them up. In normal non-stress conditions each system has a job (see fig. 3: ANS 1 on normal functions). The normal PNS is for rest, relaxation, digestion, and immobilization without fear (as when we are in the arms of one we feel close to). The SES includes social warmth, a friendly animated face, voice prosody, listening, interacting, bonding, communication, and integrated thinking and feeling. The SNS is the charged and energized state we need when we are working, exercising, or learning in an alert and engaged manner.

6. *Ladder of Dissolution*

The next chart (see fig. 5: ANS 3) emphasizes the ladder, to show how we move automatically from one system to the next in descending order *as stress increases*. Jackson discovered this hierarchical order in 1850, before we had a term or common acceptance of the dynamics of the SES.

7. *Subway Story (Dissolution Example)*

For example, you smile at a person as you scoot in next to him to take a seat on the subway. These behaviors indicate you are in the SES. Your seatmate looks annoyed and moves away from you, pulling his belongings closer to him. Then he shoves you, telling you to get away from him. You immediately react by getting angry, and saying, "hey, stop that!" Or you could get up and get as far away from him as possible. Either way you are now in the SNS in fight or flight automatic response. But say you stayed in the seat, fuming. Next, your seatmate opens his coat, grabs a knife and traps you by grabbing your throat and threatening you with the knife. You freeze, as you have no other option. You are now in PNS, life threat response.

The subway confrontation story illustrates the attempt to use SES as the first

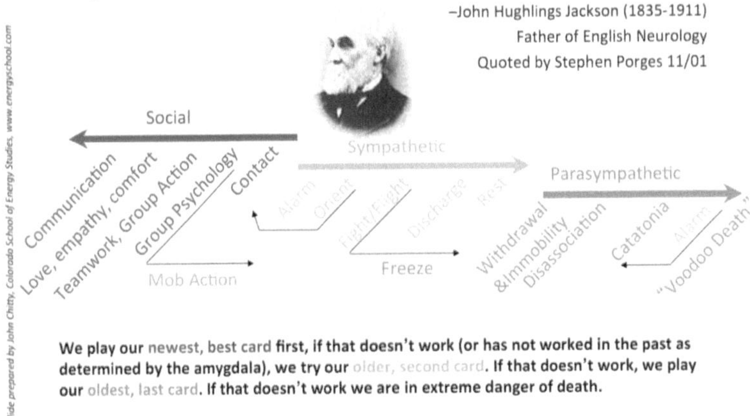

Figure 5. ANS 3

"card." When being friendly failed, the SNS (second card) was engaged. When the SNS fight response was met by a trapped feeling when the assailant pulled a weapon, the ANS dropped down immediately into the PNS as a freeze response to a life threat.

In fig. 5: ANS 3, Johnson is quoted as saying that the higher systems inhibit the lower. This means we try our best to function at a higher level. A history of trauma or abuse can weaken that capacity. This is because if we need to be constantly alert to danger and therefore spend much time in trauma states, we lose the neuroplasticity of the brain that gently calls upon the calmer, thinking brain to help us out. The safety blanket is thin and frayed, our need for love and healthy nurturing not fed. The brain prunes the branches so much that the SES is weak. However, people can increase their ability to build the SES. Once they do, it can act as an inhibitor to stop the impulsive actions of the SNS by way of the "vagal brake."

8. *The Vagal Brake*

Although dissolution pressures are automatic, the SES can stop the SNS from acting automatically at times. The impulse to strike out in the throes of anger, when brought to awareness from an "online" thinking brain (in SES), allows the SES to put the brakes on the more impulsive SNS. To use the previous scenario, the seatmate on the subway example shoves you. You flare into instant distress, while considering fight or flight (the job of the SNS to protect you). In those few seconds you scan your environment and quickly assess the dynamics including your need to stay on the subway for three more stops, the unlikely chance you could get support or protection from others on the train, the trouble you might get in if you got angry at this time. Your vigilant eyes notice the dissociated look and very disheveled dress of your assailant. You size him up as being either in shock, drugged and/or mentally compromised at this time. The SES helps you decide not to fight, to pretend like you were not bothered, to apologize in order to hopefully calm him down, and to look for any open seats away from him. Slowly you move away when you can, willing to offer a smile if he looks at you.

This is an example of the SES ventral vagal complex (VVC) using tools to stop the automatic Fight/Flight response of the SNS. You have successfully utilized the vagal brake, which acted as restraint, or brake, limiting heart rate. As Porges writes, "Inhibitory (brake) effects of the VVC branch of vagus allow for a wide range of adaptive, prosocial behaviors" (ibid., p. 69). In essence the SES can act like an "intensity controller" (Samsel, n. d.) for arousal and doing. It affects mostly the heart keeping it humming at varying paces to match the amount of energy we need as those needs shift. A decrease in ventral vagal (up into SNS) frees up energy for activity in a precise and prompt way. So, for example, one can jump up off the couch when one has been sedentary to respond to a loud sound in the next room. Like a smooth new car, this makes for fluid shifting and balance between goal related activity and social activity (ibid.).

9. *Old and New Model of ANS: Summary*

- OLD MODEL: Two: Parasympathetic (PNS) or Sympathetic (SNS) reciprocate like on a seesaw, switched on/off, like a light.
- NEW MODEL: Three: hierarchical flow (try evolutionarily newest (SES) first). This phylogenetically formed, mammalian aspect is called the "Social Engagement System" (SES).
- SES helps mammals survive by engaging in protection, attraction, and group bonding.
- SAFETY or detection of safety (neuroception) is the ONLY road to SES. Once in SES, people engage comfortably, think clearly, can best learn and create.

Aspect	Old View	New View
Importance	**Under-appreciated**	**Supreme Importance**
How many parts	**Two** (Sym-, Parasym-)	**Three** (Social, Sym-, Parasym-)
Action	**Reciprocal** (Sympathetic and Parasympathetic are seesaw, on/off)	**Sequential** based on phylogeny (evolutionarily newer vs. older)
ANS Categorization of Vagus Nerve	**All Parasympathetic**	**Mixed** (Ventral branch of Vagus is not Parasympathetic)
Therapy Goal	**Parasympathetic relaxation**	**Re-establish newer branches**
Babies	**Feel no pain and have no memory**	**ANS is hyper-sensitive & records experiences, particularly betrayals**
Popular characterization	Parasympathetic "Rest & rebuild" Sympathetic **"Fight or Flight"**	**Differentiate "normal functions" from "stress functions"**

Figure 6. Old and New Views of ANS. (Recreated from Chitty, 2013 p. 119)

C. Trauma and Polyvagal Theory

1. *Introduction*

Polyvagal theory refines our understanding of trauma. It teaches us what happens internally in the nervous system and how our underlying visceral state colors our reactions. Porges' theory is especially important for individuals and families who have experienced trauma because he normalizes the reactions people have to traumatic events. For example, dissociation is an adaptive (PNS) reaction when one is in a life-threatening situation. People can be relieved of feelings of shame to learn that their biology instinctively came up with the safest response to the danger. For example, people often wish they had gotten away when trapped by another, but they froze. They learn that their body instinctively assessed (using neuroception) that they could neither win that fight nor safely get away. When the body assesses a life threat it goes into a freeze state for the best likely outcome of survival.

2. *Stimulus – Response and PT*

Stimulus (S) information goes in and the body automatically responds (R) from the SNS, SES or PNS.

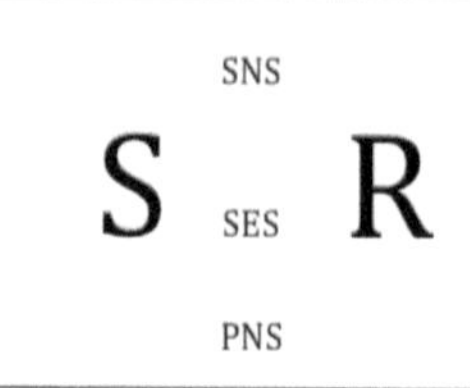

Figure 7. Stimulus-Response and Polyvagal Theory

When a person experiences chronic or severe trauma, there was often failure in the functioning of the SES, which is usually the first response to stimuli. This is likely because the traumatized person could not get the protection or help they needed to feel safe and easily recover. Disruption in their ability to access the SES for help changes brain pathways and creates a trauma response that could endure under new threats.

Samsel describes it this way:

> The result of the trauma response is a spiral of autonomic and emotional dysregulation that produces progressive damage to the organism if not reversed. The main long-term effects are perpetrated through exaggerated swings between the sympathetic fight/flight system (SNS) and the dorsal vagal 'freeze' system (PNS). The latter may have been involved as the initial response to the traumatic events, or may have been recruited as a desperate brake on the spiraling sympathetic arousal system. These alternating aspects of this dysregulation are so hard on the body that they … (can cause chronic physical illnesses or conditions). (http://reichandlowentherapy.org/content/vegetative/dorsal_shift.html)

A trauma response seems to arise when very early efforts to regulate (return to SES) after a trauma are unsuccessful. This could be because the initial trauma was so great, like when the perpetrator was also an attachment figure or there was no one else to help you return to feeling safe. It could also be because social norms precluded outside comfort or the individual physical acts and emotional expressiveness required to "shake off" the early trauma response. In either case, the result is that those who suffer chronic trauma (with minimal experience of feeling protected or safe) often have a narrow window of tolerance for disturbing stimuli, producing fluctuations between hypo-and hyper-aroused states (Ogden, Minton, & Pain, 2006).

3. *Clinical Example of Trauma Response*

a. Presenting Problem

A male adult client came into his session hyperaroused, talking about work stress and his greed to make more and more money to build his successful business and fear of failing at that. This is a common theme. I mirror him and listen to his excitement and often get hyperaroused just listening to him. He is aware of being generally hyperaroused, working very long days. However he can also down regulate (from the SNS to the PNS) with regular yoga, meditation and a spiritual practice. But he tends to go from one extreme to the other (hyper or hypo), with difficulty in the middle (the SES). His wife complains that he does not share his emotions. He says he is a good listener but does not self-disclose to others. He admires people who can self-disclose and reports therapy is the only place he can be "genuine."

He recently decided after his morning yoga, not to meditate, but to sit on the couch and spend time with his wife. She said it was nice that he listened but missed that he could not share his own feelings.

b. Intervention

To assess his level of emotional sharing and to practice (which can strengthen the communication level of the SES), I invited the client to tell me the first five feeling states he had experienced since the morning. To help out I started the sentence for him, "When I woke up I felt ..." and he added, "tired." I began again for him, "When I was driving I felt ..." and he added, "I felt anxious." He was able to do the rest himself: "in my first meeting I felt impatient, during a presentation I felt excited; dealing with a problem I felt confused." I praise him for his efforts and he visibly relaxes. Feeling confident and safe he goes deeper discussing his trauma of being in a newborn incubator. He has scars around his belly and a hole in his back. He had four surgeries before age two to repair his lower gastrointestinal tract.

c. Insight

He pauses and makes the following link himself. "My greed (at work) is not related to money, but is related to fear of failure, that I won't be enough." He shared his insight that his fear as a child relates to his fear as an adult. So he could have compassion for his fear, I illustrated walking on a tightrope over a shark tank as someone asked me my feelings. I am in SNS fear, must move to survive, no time for the emotional world of SES. All I want is to get to the other side. For homework, he planned to do some centering and grounded breathing (to feel compassion for his trauma related fear) before sharing five feelings of the day with his wife.

d. Other Somatic Based Trauma Treatment

In terms of treatment, the work of Peter Levine (2010) and David Berceli (2005) specifically targets the trauma response, in large part through activation of movement including trembling. The trembling moves energy that needs completion so the effects of trauma can be resolved or reduced. The Reich and Lowen traditions have always included the activation of movement in the concept of body armor and organismic response to negating forces. (as in the Hilton diagram, 2008).

D. Attachment and Polyvagal Theory

The securely attached child moves flexibly between all three levels, to bond and seek safety using the SES, to explore through play (SNS/SES) and to rest safely in the arms of the parent (PNS). For a visual of circles of security and insecurity see fig. 2 on p. 113 (Schroeter, 2014 BA (24) p. 105–132). The insecure patterns have a smaller window of tolerance, or narrower range of time spent in the SES and are generally organized either lower in the PNS as hypoaroused), or high in the SNS as hyperaroused (ibid., p. 118, fig. 6). They can move quickly from high to low or vice versa, because the SES range is so narrow. The goal of clinical work is to expand the range of the SES. Clinical applications will be examined next.

III. Clinical Application and Tools

A. Threat Chart and PT

The Threat Chart was created by Tina Payne Bryson (co-author of *The Whole Brain Child*) to indicate where the brain goes under states of threat.

Although this copy is in black and white, the color version is useful for visual indication of arousal movement when stimulated by real or perceived states of threat. The top (Fear, Stress etc.) is the RED ZONE. When we get angry we "turn red" and if we get very angry we may erupt. So like a thermometer the hot zone is indicated in red. The top layer refers to the SNS. The middle zone is GREEN, indicating the bright, alert, emotionally balanced nature of the SES. This is the state that is wider and easier to move back to in securely attached people. The bottom is the BLUE zone. Blue is a color that can connote sadness or depression.

Remember, there are normal functions of the RED and BLUE zones. The words printed in this chart indicate what happens to the organism when we are in those zones AS A RESPONSE TO THREAT.

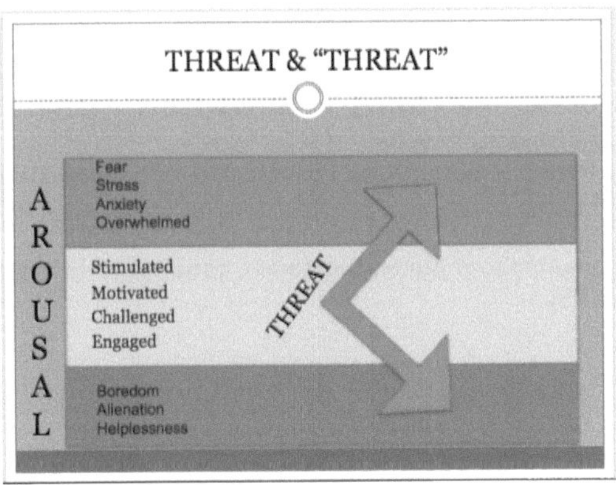

Figure 8. Threat and Arousal Chart

This chart (see fig. 8) is a simple and useful clinical tool. I have found that children as young as five years old, as well as adults can identify their arousal level. Even when they are in the RED or BLUE, where thinking functions poorly, clients can identify their arousal level. When presented with empathy and understanding, this chart becomes a tool to observe visceral states (or ANS states) and help bring clients back into the GREEN zone.

B. Arousal Zones with Normal and Stress Responses

Figure 9 combines arousal zones with cartoons of facial expressions typical of that zone. It is a tool to summarize the normal and stress functions of the ANS. Below is a clinical vignette illustrating Bioenergetic work to shift ANS states.

High-hyperarousal (SNS) THE RED ZONE
Normal: fight/flight (anger, fear); mobilization.

Under threat: Increased sensations, flooded, emotional reactivity, hypervigilance, intrusive imagery, flashbacks, disorganized cognitive processing, anxiety, impulsivity.

Optimal arousal zone (SES) THE GREEN ZONE
Normal: arousal capacity "window of tolerance"
Ventral vagal (where emotions can be tolerated and information integrated)
Calm, engaged.

Under threat: trouble communicating (move automatically to SNS, if that fails move to PNS).

Low-hypoarousal (PNS) THE BLUE ZONE
Normal: rest, relax, digest, immobilization without fear (safe in arms of another).

Under Threat: Dorsal vagal "immobilization" response, shock, relative absence of sensation; Numbing of emotions, depression, dissociation; disabled cognitive processing, reduced physical movement

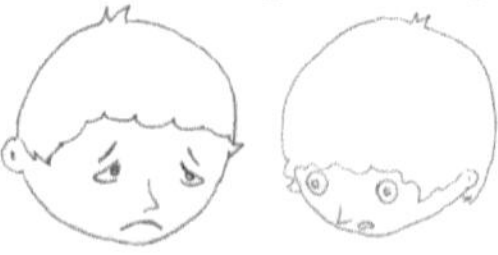

Figure 9. Chart adapted from Ogden, Minton and Pali (2006) and Corrigan, Fisher and Nutt (2010). Characters created and added by Vincentia Schroeter (2015)

1. *Case Vignette: Bioenergetic Session, WOT and ANS State Shifts*

The Window of Tolerance (WOT) is a concept coined by Dan Siegel (Siegel, 1999). A client stated her intention to solidify and expand a happy feeling she came in with by hitting with the heavy wooden bat on the mat in the office. First, she does some centering and grounding familiar to her that helps her feel gravity pull her to feeling more solid and feel her pelvis as an anchor to support her lower body. Once she has increased her charge, some pleasant shaking begins.

When she begins pounding the bat on the mat, she enjoys the movement until she hits a block in her diaphragm and throat. We do some breathing and voice work to help move through the block. As her voice is getting strong she is surprised by some anger. Next, sadness appears. She stays present (I am watching her eyes and monitoring the fluidity of her body movement to assess this level of presence). Anger comes through her eyes more as she stares at the pillow she is hitting. Discharging more anger brings the sadness to her face and her eyes droop. Opening the throat she continues with sound. Sounds change and sounds last longer. Soon sad "ohs" turn into sobbing as her diaphragm lets go. Next, she has an impulse to drop the bat, lean over and clutch a pillow. She follows these impulses and can feel her breath on the pillow, which she clutches with both hands.

Her energy has shifted. She feels contained, safer and in her words, "a new boundary" with cuddling, while leaning over the pillow. This allows deeper sobbing to emerge until she feels complete. She was surprised that opening up the charge brought anger and sadness. The mobility of engaging the SNS (using arm and back to hit) completes that movement and she drops more into affective sadness that she can own and feel good about. She has moved into the SES.

The client reports feeling more openness and reports, "I have never gone there before." This indicates that the feeling of a wider SES is pleasant and new.

C. ANS Portals and Afferent Communication

1. *Introduction*

A concept arising from Porges' work that has exciting clinical applications for somatic psychotherapists trained in anatomy is the use of *"Portals" or points of entry to affect a change in the ANS branches.* Chitty (2013) reports "ANS portals are anatomical components of the ANS that can be physically stimulated to support a particular layer. By stimulating a location in a special way, ANS change can be created" (p. 137). This means we can "reboot" the nervous system.

> "Approximately 80% of the vagal fibers are afferent (originate from the body to affect the brain) and provide important information regarding visceral state ... the vagal system becomes ... a portal to neural systems in other parts of the brain ... There is a strong neuroanatomical and neurophysiological justification to predict that stimulation of the vagal afferents would change activity of higher brain structures" (Porges, 2003).

This is very hopeful for bodyworkers and particularly somatic psychotherapists who are trained to follow the emotional aspects of changes in the nervous system. Stimulating any single afferent to the brainstem and limbic system will improve the whole nervous system. For example, Porges' ongoing research providing acoustic stimulation to autistic children improves their communication and social interaction (Porges, 2008, 2011).

Bioenergetic therapists are not traditionally trained to focus on the workings of the nervous system. We are well trained in the workings of the muscular holding patterns and their mental and emotional results, both adaptive and maladaptive. We understand mobilization, immobilization and trauma in the body quite well. We have long professed that the body speaks to the brain and not just the brain to the body. We utilize varied hands on techniques to "move energy." We see the effects of this movement of energy but perhaps can begin to describe it in a new way.

Understanding the previous principle that there are anatomical "portals" we can stimulate to affect this movement of energy in the ANS is exciting. With polyvagal theory, the nervous system comes more into view as an essential component in our work. We can use some of our techniques with a new understanding of how they affect the nervous system. Next, portals and techniques will be identified for each of the three parts of the ANS.

2. *PNS Portals*

The portal for the PNS, based on anatomy is the vagus nerve, accessible on both sides of the neck, and sacral plexus (L4–S4), which provides motor and sensory nerves for posterior thigh, lower leg, foot and part of the pelvis. Look at *figure 3* to see where PNS nerves innervate (stimulate to action). Notice the many fibers sub (below) the diaphragm, indicating the lower part of the body, as well as some in the neck area. Therefore contact with the neck and lower back (lumbar-sacral area) will stimulate the PNS and help restore it's functions. For example, when you stretch your neck gently or get a neck massage it is often very relaxing. Relaxation is the royalty of the PNS. Contact with the lower back (lower lumbar and sacral regions) can innervate the lower body, including the pelvic area (relaxes the perineum), increases peristalsis (digestion) and restores normal bladder and rectal function. Again, we have to be relaxed for digestion and elimination to function optimally.

3. *PNS Portal Technique*

This reminds me of two touch techniques that Mae Nascimento (2014) introduced in her article (BA, 24,11–31). The point of her paper was to utilize techniques that "create a more introspective nature, helping the connection with the energy flow" (ibid., p. 29). Because they address the PNS, I will quote from her paper here:

> A. LUMBAR TOUCH
>
> The therapist must be at the client's side so that he can observe his reactions and ask him from time to time what is going on.
>
> With the client in a grounding position (standing with knees slightly bent), stand behind the client and touch the lumbar zone of the vertebral column between the fourth and fifth vertebrae with the index and middle fingers and the palm of your hand facing down toward the floor. The client is asked to breathe so that he can keep the focus upon what happens within himself.
>
> 'It is a physical touch … that reaches the energetic flow through the nervous system and not through the bone structure or muscular layers … this touch activates the energy through the autonomous nervous system and by resonance over the sensory and emotional fields. It also activates the perineum and the Hara*, facilitating an internal grounding and a deep plunging within oneself' (Basso & Pulstilnik, 2001, p. 49–50).
>
> (*Centro Hara – by which the mother's blood fed us through the umbilical cord and where we get our blood nutrition through our digestive process (Basso & Pulstilnik, 2001, p. 50).
>
> B. CERVICAL TOUCH
>
> With the client in a standing grounded position, touch very gently with your middle finger the base of the neck in the occipital foramen, before the first cervical vertebrae. Your hand will be facing down toward the floor.
>
> 'This touch must be done with the conscious intention of activating the innervation of the cranial parasympathetic which innervates the arms, lungs and heart.

The aim is to relax the ego control in a way to help the person plunge into his inner being and to get more conscious' (ibid, p. 57).

It is important for the therapist to note the position of the hands in each touch because they have to be turned toward the same direction of the energy flow (down in both cases) (p. 27–29).

4. SNS Portals

In the SNS branch the muscles of the limbs (to run or fight or reach) and the spine (to mobilize for quick action) are innervated (see SNS nerves toward back (dorsal) part of body in figure 3). This is very familiar to Bioenergetic Analysts who have many techniques to help mobilize blocked affect toward active expression, including kicking, hitting, reaching and expressing emotions, that might be blocked and frozen by the PNS.

5. SNS Portals and Catharsis

Some have argued against catharsis (venting a large build up of emotion) as a viable therapy technique claiming it "floods" the system and that the results are "temporary," and therefore not valuable. Peter Levine *(In an Unspoken Voice)* concludes that repeated emotional expression in a cathartic manner (screaming, pounding pillows, etc.) results in release of endorphins, which could be addictive. He touts body awareness over catharsis.

Here is a counter argument from an ANS lens. It is true that under stress, the hyperactive arousal of the SNS can cause acting out of violent aggression from uncontained anger, high levels of agitation, anxiety to a level of panic, and/or fear that overwhelms the person. But in Bioenergetics we show people safe and focused ways to express anger that is not chaotic.

When we use techniques to move the fear or anger through by expressive work, the client does not get stuck in an SNS level. Once they complete a need to express blocked affect, their system feels better and they are no longer flooded. When emotional release happens one automatically moves from the SNS to the SES. They naturally move into the happier, more social SES where the oxytocin and vasopressin (love hormones) contribute to a renewed openness and positive outlook. The new neural pathways for being in the SES are strengthened and can expand the WOT, meaning they feel rewarded for being in the SES zone and the compulsion to act out from the SNS reduces.

In Levine's view, "There is an addictive quality ... that we are drawn to create and re-create" (p. 70). I think he is referring to people (he admits he himself re-created addictive bad relationships) (ibid.) who are organized in hyperarousal and have trouble containing anger. But if one spends more time in the SES, where the whole brain, both thinking and feeling is online, rather than in the SNS, where the compulsion to react to danger by fight or flight is so strong, then the person has more choices. For example, a person feels threatened and gets angry. They feel the impulse to yell at someone they love (in SNS). They take a few breaths, access (strengthened by neural pathways) the SES, use the brain to quickly decide, "I don't want to hurt anyone" and instead of blowing up they go to the gym to move the anger through. They leave the gym with a flood of endorphins, which makes them feel good in a healthy way.

6. *SNS Portal Techniques*

a. Grounding

Bioenergetic therapists are trained in observing the energy of the body, including where there is movement and lack of movement in the chronic (usually unconscious) holding patterns of the body. Before activating an expression of fear or anger or reaching that might be blocked, clients are invited to do some form of grounding, which can happen in the relationship (e.g. the therapist making the client feel seen, heard and cared for) and/or internally by opening to the pull of gravity to make one feel centered and therefore have more room for a fuller, more congruent expression. In terms of portals, the SNS is innervated in the dorsal (back) of the body. Grounding helps one feel one's stance as more grounded. Classic grounding techniques involve rolling the feet over a ball or dowel, leaning on one leg or the other, jumping down, a forward bend, with slow roll up. For detail figures and explanations on classic Bioenergetic techniques see Schroeter and Thomson (2011) *Bend Into Shape, Techniques for Bioenergetic Therapists.*

b. Activating the SNS

The large muscles, especially the arms and legs are the portals to stimulate active expression (to complete a running away or fighting impulse) from the SNS. This is the realm very familiar to Bioenergetic therapists. From a polyvagal viewpoint, if a client is in the most primitive level, in the stress of the PNS, they could be in danger if they are very depressed or dissociative for an extended time. The danger of staying there too long is to disorganize. If you assess they need to mobilize some aggression, then moving these big muscles could bring energy that moves them into the more energized SNS.

c. Technique

Have a client (after grounding) stomp his/her feet, kick a cube, punch a pillow, hit with a bat or racquet, yell, "No" or other angry sounds. By contrast, if the impulse that needs completion is fear-based, the person can run in place and scream or push away with their arms.

i. Case example: I had a five-year-old client who told his mother he was going to "jump out the window and kill myself." The Mom was distressed because she expected him to be "my happy little boy" even though the boy was upset because the parents were getting a divorce. I brought out a box with wooden balls that had to be hammered vigorously with the wooden mallet to go in the holes. This little boy hammered those balls for 40 minutes! Afterward his Mom reported he could verbalize, "I am mad that you sent Dad away." When Mom validated his anger, he said, "I love you."

ii. PT analysis: This child was in the shock and depression of the PNS, making suicidal threats (jump out of the window). Any input that improves our ability to orient and communicate will inhibit the stress response. By orienting to the present in finding bright colored wooden balls to hit, and by my verbal encouragement the boy moved out of the PNS depressive state. Activating his arms and hands to pound the wooden balls moved him up into the SNS. After that expression was complete (and accepted by Mom) he could move to the SES and verbally express his feelings of both anger and love.

7. Bringing Down Anxiety with the Vagal Brake

The vagal system, according to Porges is a feedback system with motor pathways, sensory pathways and brain pathways to regulate motor output. The vagus nerve acts to *inhibit the sympathetics (SNS).* Since the SNS is set to run in overdrive all the time (due to our constant scanning for any perceived or real danger), health depends on an active *vagal brake.* As stated earlier the job of vagal brake is for the SES to stop this constant high level of adrenalized alertness.

Thayer and Lane (2000) as reported in "Cranial Intelligence blog" (Steve Haines, October 4, 2010) show that ANS imbalance (causing anxiety, poor attention and immune disorders ...) is due to low vagal tone. This means the vagal brake is not working well. It would be like needing new brake shoes for the car. The vagal brake not working causes the SNS to be disinhibited. Like hitting the car in front of you from behind when your brakes do not stop soon enough, SNS dominance creates disasters to self and often clashes with others. This dominance causes the system to be less flexible in its responses. The following is a Bioenergetic technique to access the vagal brake.

8. *SNS Portal Technique to Access the Vagal Brake*

To move from the overactive SNS, which is focused externally and innervates the big muscles for action, one needs to activate interoceptive (internal) signals to access the SES. So accessing the heart and the gut are helpful in inhibiting the SNS. We can use the terms "gut brain" or "belly brain" and "heart brain" less as a metaphor and more as a reality, since Porges has shown how the body sends messages afferently from these parts of the body directly to the brain. If the client makes regular use of some type of relaxation and focusing technique, they can grease the wheels so that they can slide more quickly out of the SNS when stuck there. Make sure the vigilant SNS dominated client feels safe before attempting the following Bioenergetic technique:

a. Invite the client to close his/her eyes and relax the back by lying down or sitting propped against pillows, where they can feel their back. If SNS flexor muscles are switched on (readiness to strike or move), lying down or relaxing the back sends a signal to the spine, (which is a portal to the SNS), to reduce that flexion. As the client feels his/her back with support, the flexors relax and the more receptive extensor muscles are engaged.
b. Next, place your hands (or have the client place his/her hands) on their heart and belly (abdomen) and have them breathe into each area, to observe and relax. The open heart and relaxed belly can inhibit the SNS. Follow the energy to see if they can deepen the breath or have a need to move toward some affect.

9. *SES Portals*

For the social or communication branch (SES) of the ANS, cranial nerves V, VII, IX, X and XI are the portals. See in figure 3 the nerves going toward the ventral (front) of the body supra (above) the diaphragm and from the neck toward the heart and thus innervating all our expressive and communication modes such as hearing, seeing, speaking and animated emotion. The motor outputs of the SES according to Porges are head turning, muscles of facial expression, muscles of mastication (chewing), middle ear muscles, larynx and pharynx, heart and bronchi. The sensory inputs (portals) to the SES cranial nerves are interoception (from inside, especially heart and gut messages), sound (it changes the tension in the middle ear muscles), mucosal linings of oral, nasal cavities, the sinuses, the teeth and the cranium (skull).

10. SES Techniques

The cranial nerves as a group can be used by gently stimulating their sensory and motor components in the face, throat and neck (Chitty, 2013, p. 137). Here are some examples of using various SES portals. Once open, follow the energy and see if it expands the SES or moves into the PNS (maybe due to a need to cry or grieve) or SNS (due to a need for movement toward expressing fear or anger).

a. OPENING THE HEART: Have the client think of someone they love and have them reach toward that person (or a pet). This induces warm feelings and releases the bonding hormones, oxytocin and vasopressin, which are in the SES.
b. OPENING THE VOICE: Have the person vocalize words, songs, or emotional expressions. Join them in those sounds if it makes them feel safer or is playful. (Play involves creativity. Interpersonal play expands the SES).
c. MAKING FACES: Have the client move the muscles of their face around to loosen facial and eye muscles. Open and close the mouth to loosen the jaw. Next, have them imitate and exaggerate expressions of anger, disgust, worry, fear, anger, sadness, shyness, happiness and joy. Use any variety. If they begin to laugh, this loosens the belly and diaphragm, which is also in the SES.
d. MASSAGING THE HEAD OR NECK: The tenth cranial nerve is the origin of the vagus. Any neck massage can stimulate the area. Massage of the skull can calm the hot head of someone stuck in a SNS stress response.

   EXAMPLE: I saw the following scene. A woman was spinning in anger and agitated worry, repeating over and over what was bothering her with no resolution. Her husband instinctively went toward her, placed one hand on the back of her head as his other hand covered her forehead and the top of her head. It was almost like a containing helmet. He made a joke, "Heal!" This made her laugh and immediately the overheated spinning monologue dropped away. He looked at her warmly. She smiled back, sharing in his humor and warmth. She had returned to the SES.

D. Summary of PT Implications for Clinicans

1. An overall therapeutic goal is to re-establish the Social Engagement System, because it is the most sophisticated in repairing stress. This may occur by completing thwarted movements in the SNS or the PNS.
2. If you can identify what state of the ANS the client is currently in, you will have a road map to help him or her.
3. It is important to convey to the client that wherever they are in the ANS is adaptive for them.
4. Keep in mind that when the newer Social Engagement (SES) fails, then the natural strategy is to go (automatically) to the SNS, if not successful there, then to the PNS.
5. Provide clients with a visual of the three branches to help them identify where they are in the ANS.
6. Be aware of your voice prosody and facial expression to help invite clients into the SES, where they will feel safest and therefore most cooperative.
7. To be the most present as a therapist, you need to be aware of your own ANS state and practice self-care when moving out of the SES.

E. Summary of PT Implications for *Somatic* Clinicans

1. An overall therapeutic goal is to re-establish the SES, i.e., "reclaim a natural, childlike state of joy" (1995, p. 10).
2. Identify the current state of ANS using body observations and interpersonal reactions. Is the client in the SNS, SES, or PNS?
3. Being stuck in the SNS or PNS means they are feeling threatened and not safe. To shift from stressed PNS or stressed SNS, activate deep breathing. Notice where the energy is stuck.
4. Use somatic interventions to help move energy from one state to another.
5. Use knowledge of ANS portals to inform your somatic and relational interventions.
6. Activate emotional expression to move blocked affect. Grounded anger work mobilizes the SNS. Once discharged, the client naturally moves into

social openness of the SES or rests calmly in the PNS. No shift indicates energy is stuck and the client may not feel safe enough to shift levels at this time. Frame this as a protective impulse of neuroception.

7. CAUTION: The immobilization of the PNS may be adaptive. Help the client feel safe by mirroring their affect and keeping a safe distance unless invited to help mobilize them. Remind them to orient to the current environment and use it to feel as safe as they can. Helping the client move from the stress response (immobilization) to the normal response (rest and recover) of the PNS may help them recover their balance.
8. Become aware of your own signs for moving out of the SES, because the SES is the best level to be in when seeing clients. Valuable self-care techniques are provided in the article, "Bioenergetic Self-Care for Therapists" (Heinrich-Clauer, 2015, BA (25) p. 41–72).

IV. Conclusion

This paper introduced the tenants of polyvagal theory to somatic psychotherapists for the benefit of utilizing the concepts in their clinical work. The concept of neuroception helps therapists appreciate that any action or behavior by a client can be seen as a response to perceived or real danger. Identifying which of the three (SES, SNS, PNS) branches of the ANS the client is in can create a roadmap for interventions. The dissolution from newer to older states helps the therapist understand the neurobiology of affect regulation. Somatic psychotherapists in general and Bioenergetic therapists in particular can use their knowledge of the how the body both expresses and inhibits affect to aid clients in moving through ANS states and expand their capacity for utilizing the SES.

As Pat Ogden writes, "The body speaks clearly to those who know how to listen" (p. 25). While Bioenergetics has always attended to the non-verbal, body-based, implicit processes over verbal explicit processes, polyvagal theory helps us elucidate this language of the body from the point of the nervous system. The body dramatically reveals the three levels of the ANS and shows us visually the shifts between them. Seeing these shifts has always been a nuanced skill from the Bioenergetic toolkit. However, we now have language to label these shifts in a new way. Stephen Porges' immense contribution to psychophysiological understanding by the introduction of polyvagal theory, gives us a complete map of the ANS. We can now incorporate that map into our clinical understanding and practice.

This paper is an attempt to invite others to ride the wave as it crests. I expect the tipping point to come, where all somatic psychotherapists will easily communicate in ANS terms. This neurophysiological lens aids us in feeling compassion for clients by understanding their behavior in a new light. It can reduce shame in clients by helping them understand their biology from the polyvagal point of view. Incorporating lessons from neuroscience like polyvagal theory into practice strengthens the validity of our work by grounding it in sound science.

References

Berceli, D. (2005) *Trauma releasing exercises: revolutionary new method for stress/trauma recovery.* Book Surge Publishing.

Chitty, J. (2013), *Dancing with yin and yang: ancient wisdom, modern psychotherapy and Randolph Stone's polarity therapy.* Colorado: Polarity Press.

Clauer, J. (2011), Neurobiology and psychological development of grounding and embodiment. *Bioenergetic Analysis*, (21), 17–55.

Eichhorn, N. (2012), Safety: the preamble for social engagement: interview with Stephen Porges. In *Somatic Psychotherapy Today, 1*(4).

Heinrich-Clauer, V. (2015). Bioenergetic self-care for therapists. *Bioenergetic Analysis* 25, 41–72.

Hilton, R. (2008) *Relational somatic psychotherapy.* M. Seick (Ed.) S. B.Grad.Inst.

Levine, P. (2010), *In an unspoken voice: how the body releases trauma and restores goodness.* North Atlantic Books.

Lowen, A. (1975), *Bioenergetics.* New York: Coward, McCann & Geoghen Inc.

Lowen, A. (1995), *Joy, surrender to the body and to life.* New York: Penguin Books.

Marucheau, L. (2015) Power point for Interpersonal Neurobiology study group

Ogden, Minton, & Pain (2006) *Trauma and the body.* New York, NY: WW Norton & Company.

Ogden, P. (2013), *Sensorimotor psychotherapy: interventions for trauma and attachment.* New York: Norton.

Panksepp, J. Biven, L. (2012), *The archaeology of mind: neuroevolutionary origins of human emotions.* New York: Norton.

Porges, SW. (1995), Orienting in a defensive world: mammalian modifications of our evolutionary heritage. A polyvagal theory. *Psychophysiology, 32*, 301–318.

Porges, SW. (2011), *The polyvagal theory: neurophysiological foundations of emotions, attachment, communication, self-regulation.* New York: Norton.

Reich, W. (1933), *Character analysis.* Vienna: Psychoanalytic Press

Schroeter, V, Thomson, B. (2011), *Bend into shape, techniques for bioenergetic therapists.* Self-published. Encinitas, CA.

Samsel, M. (n. d.) Shift Toward the Social Engagement System *www.reichandlowentherapy.com*

Siegel, D. J., Bryson,T. (2011), *The whole-brain child.* Random House.

Spencer, H. (1864) *Principles of biology.* New York. Prometheus Books.

Thayler & Lane (2000), in Cranial Intelligence Blog. Haines, S. (10.4.2010).

About the Author

Vincentia Schroeter, PhD, is a licensed psychotherapist in private practice in Escondido, California and on the teaching faculty of the Southern California Institute of Bioenergetic Analysis (SCIBA). She is a member of the IIBA faculty, chief editor of the IIBA journal and co-author with Barbara Thomson of the Bioenergetics techniques manual, Bend Into Shape.

Vincentia Schroeter
E-mail: vincentiaschroeter@gmail.com
www.vincentiaschroeterphd.com

On Falling, Holding, and Grounding

Gerald Perlman

> "Grasping is the source of all our problems. Since impermanence to us spells anguish, we grasp on to things desperately, even though all things change. We are terrified of letting go; terrified, in fact, of living at all, since learning to live is learning to let go. And this is the tragedy and the irony of our struggle to hold on: Not only is it impossible, but it brings us the very pain we are seeking to avoid."
>
> *Sogyal Rinpoche, Feb. 2, 2014*

Abstracts

English

Building on the theoretical and developmental history of the *fear of falling, holding* and *grounding* in bioenergetic analysis and other psychodynamic theories, this paper presents some of the expressions, experiences and anxieties of falling and the defensive/adaptive, characterological, intra-psychic and interpersonal correlates of holding. In addition the importance of grounding is discussed for setting a foundation and a space/relationship in which it feels safe enough to surrender to the fear of falling. This yields to one's understanding of the need to *hold,* in whatever adaptive form it takes, in order to maintain attachments and protect the life force within.

Key words: bioenergetic analysis, early trauma, fear of falling, grounding, hang-ups, holding.

German

Aufbauend auf der theoretischen und entwicklungsbezogenen Geschichte der Fallangst, des Haltens und des Erdens in der Bioenergetischen Analyse und anderen psychodynamischen Theorien, zeigt dieser Beitrag einige Ausdrucksweisen, Erfahrungen und Ängste vor dem Fallen auf sowie die defensiv-adaptiven, charakterologischen, intra-psychischen und interpersonellen Korrelate des Haltens. Zusätzlich wird die Bedeutung des Erdens für die Etablierung eines Fundaments, einer Beziehung zum Raum diskutiert, wo es sich sicher genug anfühlt, sich auf die Angst vor dem Fallen einzulassen. Das führt zu einem Verständnis der Notwendigkeit zu halten, welche Form auch immer dieses Bedürfnis annimmt, um Bindungen aufrechtzuerhalten und die innere Lebenskraft zu schützen.

French

Cet article est élaboré à partir des concepts historiques issus de l'analyse bioénergétique et d'autres théories psychodynamiques, concernant la *peur de tomber*, le fait de *se retenir* ("holding"), et l'*enracinement* ("grounding"). Il présente quelques unes des expressions, des expériences et des angoisses relatives au fait de tomber, mais également les manifestations défensives/adaptatives, caractérologiques, intrapsychiques et interpersonnelles relatives au fait de se retenir. L'importance de l'enracinement est également discutée afin de poser les bases, dans ses aspects également spatiaux et relationnels, à partir desquelles il est possible de s'abandonner à la peur de tomber tout en éprouvant une sécurité suffisante. Cela conduit au fait de mieux comprendre la nécessité que chacun éprouve dans le fait de se retenir, de quelque manière adaptative que ce soit, afin de préserver ses attachements et les forces de vie qu'ils recèlent.

Spanish

Partiendo de la historia teórica y de desarrollo del *miedo de caer, sostenimiento y arraigamiento* en el análisis bioenergético y otras teorías psicodinámicas, este documento presenta algunas de las expresiones, experiencias y ansiedades de caer y la correlación defensivo/adaptativo, caracterológica, intrapsíquica e interpersonal del sostenimiento. Además se trata la importancia del arraigamiento para establecer una fundación y un espacio/relación en la que uno se sienta lo suficientemente seguro como para rendirse ante el temor de caer. Esto cede paso al entendimiento de la necesidad de personal de *sostener*, en cualquier forma de adaptación, con el fin de preservar los apegos y proteger la fuerza vital interior.

Portuguese

Com base na história teórica e de desenvolvimento do *medo de cair, da contenção e do grounding*, na Análise Bioenergética e outras teorias psicodinâmicas, este artigo apresenta algumas expressões, experiências e ansiedades de cair e os correlatos defensivos/adaptativos, caracterológicos, intrapsíquicos e interpessoais da contenção. Além da importância do *grounding,* discute-se o estabelecimento de uma base e um espaço/relação que forneça segurança suficiente para permitir a entrega ao medo de cair. Isto leva à compreensão da necessidade da *contenção*, qualquer que seja sua forma adaptativa, no sentido de manter apegos e proteger a força de vida interior.

1. Introduction

Several years ago, before I was exposed to bioenergetic analysis, a perfect storm of events occurred in my life. My adult daughter fell into a clinical depression, which worried, scared and shamed me. I felt overwhelmed by a couple I was treating in therapy that I feared might wind up on the front page of the New York Post, ending with one of them going to jail, and my having to bear witness to their rage and disintegration in a court of law, as their two-year old child was used as a pawn between them. I was also struggling with whether or not to retire and my computer had crashed sending me into a state of panic. In addition, I had developed a profoundly painful sinus infection, which rendered me dizzy. One evening, around the time all this was bombarding my psyche, I woke up in the middle of the night to urinate. I felt disoriented and experienced a profound loss of balance and struggled to hold onto the walls, lest I fall. I felt terrified. Even as I was struggling to "hold on, hold tight and hold together," to gather my wits about me, (the default adaptive mode I use to negotiate life) I began to descend into a vortex of an agitated depression, which lasted several months.

In this state of what felt like total collapse, I sought out Scott Baum for a consultation. One of the first things he said to me was that he was a bioenergetic analyst and he noticed that my body looked like it was in a collapsed state, and that my stomach felt rigidly held in. As he inquired about this, I revealed that I always held in my stomach. This was a typical holding pattern for me. It indicated that I could take it. No matter what came my way I could stomach it. But at that moment I felt that I couldn't take it anymore and that I shouldn't have to. Because Scott was seeing my partner in therapy at the time, he suggested I see Bob Lewis whose love, humor, presence and compassion have filled me and held me more than I can say in words.

I spent months screaming in anguish, crying, raging and grieving for, among other things, the child within that had to "hold back" his own life force because of the threat that energy and soul presented to my depressed, bitter, controlling and sadistic mother and my equally sadistic, detached and narcissistic father.

Because of his work on "cephalic shock" (Lewis, 1984), Bob was particularly attuned to how my wits, at the expense of my impoverished soul and body, had helped me survive a very damaging upbringing. One day, as I was lying on the couch in his office, Bob held my head, as he had done many times before. He began gently rocking my head from left to right and asking me to let out whatever sounds I could. The rocking increased as did the pitch and intensity of the sounds I was making. These sounds resonated through my body. He accelerated the rocking motion and suddenly I felt totally disorganized, shock waves were coursing through my body and I was screaming from the depth of my soul: "I'm falling, I'm falling. Help me." I was screaming in terror as I experienced myself falling through space with no end in sight. Bob, who had been seated next to me, immediately stood up, grabbed my arm, told me to hold his arm, put his hand on my chest and said: "I am here. I have you. I'm holding you. You're safe."

I did feel truly held and safe. I understood on the deepest level, the terror of my childhood and why I had to dissociate that experience. My breathing eventually returned to a regulated state and Bob said: "Now you know what Winnicott meant about a holding environment. You didn't have one." I laughed and cried. I was exhausted but relieved and felt a little more whole and connected to my body than I had ever known before. What I had known intellectually from years of analysis was now known in a way I had never experienced before. It was no longer a cerebral understanding, it was in my body. My body tingled with that profound knowledge. It was clearer to me than ever; time does not heal those wounds that occur early in life, nor does an intellectual understanding of those early experiences devoid of affective-bodily integration. Time may conceal them, but those traumas and the bodily adaptation to them are buried within the muscles, bones, organs and every cell of our bodies. Some of us armor and hold our bodies in such a way for fear of falling, which may translate into the fear of experiencing severe anxiety, terror, depression, disorganization or rage often associated with a profound absence of a holding environment. This then tells a fuller story of our adaptations to what the Greek word trauma signifies: the wounds, damages and defeats we experienced at a time when we were not at all prepared to protect ourselves.

I have been using the words hold, holding and held to describe the physical act of tightening my stomach muscles to hold in that region in order to maintain my characterological pattern that, however ultimately limiting, protected my sense of self from being overwhelmed. I have also used the terms to denote the experience of being held by and/or holding on to another, exemplified by Bob Lewis's holding me and my holding his arm as I experienced the terror of falling forever. In the latter experience, touch became a means of feeling safely attached rather than abused. All of these holding experiences involve somato-psychic relational connections. Throughout the remainder of the paper the reader will note these various uses and meanings of the terms hold, holding, and/or held as they refer to being cared for by another or by self, or armoring and positioning oneself in relation to a real or perceived environmental invasion, neglect and/or abuse. Clearly some forms of holding are loving, encouraging, and supportive; and when they are, we feel safe enough to allow ourselves the right to reach out to or fall into the arms of another. Other forms of holding can be used to constrain, to control, to abuse, to invade, etc. We also construct our own holding patterns in order to resist falling in on ourselves, thus avoiding experiencing the realities of our embodied being, including disappointing, humiliating, terrorizing, neglectful, oppressive and/or disorganizing experiences.

As a result of Scott's observation of my holding pattern and Bob's facilitating my body awareness of and his compassionately bearing witness to my lack of a "holding environment" and my terror of "falling forever," I became fascinated with issues and experiences surrounding the "holding/falling" dialectic. As I begin to be more comfortable linking my newly formed bioenergetic awareness with my more familiar interpersonal/psychodynamic understanding, I have been asking my patients to participate in grounding exercises. I am learning that a good number of them, when I have asked them to stand on their feet, soften their knees and keep their feet parallel to each other at about shoulder width and imagine roots growing from the soles of their feet and burrowing through the ground until the roots reach the earth below, spontaneously announce that they are afraid of falling. As they leave their adaptive, protective stance, they report feeling unbalanced and in danger of falling.

2. Bioenergetic Views on Holding and Falling

Lowen (1976) has written about "hang-ups" which represent conscious or unconscious emotional conflicts that become structured in the body in the form of chronic muscular tensions, and which are the antitheses of being grounded. The further the person is from feeling grounded the greater is his hang up and fear of falling. Lowen states that the major thrust of bioenergetic work is to get a person into his legs and feet; to be truly rooted in reality means to be embodied, to be aware of one's body in space, externally and internally and in relation to others. But coming downward into one's legs/feet and thus into reality may bring with it a variety of anxieties that had been held out of awareness. Lowen talks about the fear of collapsing into a depression as one's illusions give way to the real self. The letting go of illusions, masks, and/or armor often creates a sense of loss. In his discussion of the narcissistic style, Johnson (1987) points out that as the false self of the narcissist yields to the symptomatic self, depression often follows. Lowen (1983), a self-proclaimed phallic narcissist, may have been referring to his own experience of depression as he tried to become more grounded. I recall during a first year class in bioenergetics, Jodi Schneider guiding me through the Bend-over exercise. As I rushed to return to an upright position, she cautioned me to come up slowly. As I did, a surprising wave of sadness swept through my body. No wonder I wanted to come up quickly. I had let go of the muscles in my abdomen, upper body, neck, jaw and head. When I let go of my holding pattern, the reality of a deeper grief became apparent. This is not to say that all character types/styles will experience depression or sadness as they move toward greater grounding; it may be more related to those with predominantly narcissistic styles. Others may feel anxiety, panic, rage, terror, or even joy.

Lowen (1976) posits that the fear of getting into one's real self is associated with the dread of falling. He states that "in the interval between letting go and feeling one's feet solid on the ground, one experiences the sensation of falling and the anxiety it evokes" (p. 198). In his autobiography (2003), he reiterates "all neurotic individuals have a fear of falling, because this is experienced as a defeat by the ego" (p. 180). Lowen notes that the fear of falling is also a transitional stage between being hung up and having one's feet firmly planted on the ground. In *Fear of Life* (1980) he writes that "when a patient gives up his defensive position, he will experience some sense of being mad or crazy" (p. 145).

This is not unlike the Rogerian therapist, Sidney Jourard's (1968) discussion of change in the course of psychotherapy. He posits that if one insists on holding onto the illusion one has about herself, she will clearly not grow. In letting go of the false self, there is a fear of going out of one's mind. Because indeed, for change to occur one must go out of one's illusory mind and into one more deeply grounded in reality. It resonates with Fritz Perls's famous statement challenging one to go out of her mind and into her senses. This may be terrifying. For those suffering from very early chronic trauma, letting go can signify annihilation.

Extending both Lowen's and Jourard's contention that the fear of falling is a transitional period between holding onto a familiar adaptive pattern and a letting go toward a more grounded position in reality, I am positing that each character structure, as suggested below by Hilton (2007) and Johnson (1994), has a specific holding pattern protecting one from a specific fear of falling; and that for each character structure the fear of falling may equate to the fear of re-living the dreadful dissociated embodied experiences resulting from the negative environmental forces that presented obstacles to the developmental task at hand. The fear of falling has a particular significance at each developmental level. A few examples from my practice may be useful to illustrate the point.

Case Example 1

Maggie is a very talented teacher and writer who exemplifies the schizoid structure. She came to see me when she was 67 years old, shortly after her husband of many years had died following a long illness. She appeared frightened, mousy and hid herself on the sofa in my office as far from where I sat as possible. She would often hide her face behind her hand when speaking of something uncomfortable. She told me it was her way of thinking. When she left the room at the end of a session, it seemed as if she were trying to leave without being seen. Initially, I felt weighed down by her lack of energy. But I noticed that she wore an ankle bracelet, and she had a sense of style. And when she took her hand away from her face, her eyes would connect with mine for just a second. I could feel an energy that wanted to be freed.

Grounding exercises, writing short stories about her early life experiences and connecting with a fitness trainer who comes to her apartment, all help to bring her more in touch with her body and allow more energy to be taken in, acknowledged and expressed.

During the course of our work together, she would from time to time say that she felt as if she were *falling off a cliff*, particularly when she was alone. This was a very frightening experience for her. She talked about spending more time alone and going into places that she called "unrealness, aloneness, and disembodiment." It mirrored experiences from her childhood. We talked about her experiences of being the good girl, the obedient child, and the non-expressive and non-demanding child who sort of floated around the house in which she lived with her mother, grandparents and uncle.

I noticed her feet and ankles as she spoke about these experiences. They would shake and then curl and contract. She recalled how her uncle had a foot tic, as the family called it, and about which her grandfather was furious. I suggested it might have been one of the only means of expressing the life within, (and perhaps the inhibited rage) that he had available, but his foot shaking was disdained and disallowed. No wonder she felt disembodied, she had to empty herself out and get into her head to survive. We did ankle exercises recommended by Conger (1994), which allowed a gentle layering of tolerable amounts of energy and a growing sense of groundedness as her ankles opened to her feet and calves.

Maggie talked about feeling insubstantial and of little value. We explored a childhood where she was the little adult who had to stay under the radar. Energy had to be suppressed as she tried to survive in a life-deadening environment. She never knew quite where she belonged. Her estranged father, whom her mother divorced when Maggie was 4 years old, had much energy but was seen as "being the limit," meaning "too much" in her mother's lexicon. He was a dreamer, a gambler and a risk taker.

She told a story of two college professors who wanted to work with her on an honors paper in an area of great interest to her. She chose neither of them and went to another professor for mentorship. One she didn't particular like, nor was he particularly interested in the subject matter most dear to her. When I asked about that, she told me that she was afraid that if she got too close to either of the first two they would see right through her and notice that there was nothing there. Or perhaps they would not like what they did see. She grieved missed opportunities. She spoke of how she would, until recently, hide out in groups, avoid asking for what she wanted, and make herself disappear. She referred to her childhood home as one of "stoic disappointment." She felt her family was seemingly benign to her, but devoid of energy, connection or hope. Of course we could see in the incident with her uncle's so-called foot tic, her grandfather was hardly benign. As she spoke of these experiences, I felt a heaviness across my chest and an accompanying deep sadness. When I told her of this, she excitedly said, "Me too." I then asked her to breathe into her chest. I did likewise and had an immediate reaction. As my chest filled with energy, I felt: "Oh, I exist! I am real!" I shared that experience with her. A smile came across her face, there was no hand hiding it, and she said she could feel her realness too. She laughed.

As I inquired more about her experience of falling off a cliff, she would get teary and let me know that there would be nobody to even notice that she was falling. It was frightening and terrifying and profoundly sad. She would shudder. This experience is captured in Michael Eigen's concept of an "electrified tightrope" on which the person walks with no net beneath them (Scott Baum, personal communication).

There was no one to bounce off, no borders, no boundaries; "I had no direction," she decried. The only imperative she could recall was that she and her family were not to think that "they were somebody," meaning too big for their britches; the caveat however, speaks volumes.

Maggie has come to appreciate and to know her own power and capacity for tapping into the energy available. She can hide out if she needs to, but she doesn't feel she absolutely has to anymore. She recently told me that she feels more real. It is not necessarily good or bad, just real and that is satisfying to her, she says.

Case Example 2

A 53 year old man named Dan, who fits the description of the narcissistic character structure, informed me that he had *fallen* on hard times and was depressed, his reason for seeking therapy. Hard times meant that he went from having 15 million dollars in the bank to having less than 7 million and wasn't sure how he was going to return to his former state of glory, as he put it. Nor was he anymore the "wunder kind" he had always seen himself as. He had been in a powerful executive position in a business that folded and he was consumed with getting back on top. He would often use the term: *"How the mighty have fallen!"* in reference to himself. This is a man whose mother, now deceased, told him that he was better than his sister, that she could rely on him and that she had great expectations for him. Indeed, he was a gifted, ambitious and a hard working entrepreneur, more gifted than his father. He had little respect for his wife or kids and valued himself as an honest businessman. "If only I had been more ruthless," he would lament, meaning he then wouldn't be in the circumstances in which he now found himself. He had no sense of how ruthless and disdainful he was to his family members and those who challenged his authority.

In the course of exploring his phrase, "How the mighty have fallen," I asked him to imagine himself falling from a great height. After several attempts, he was able to picture himself falling from a high place and his breathing seemed to stop for a moment. For a very brief second, I could see a rise and a tightening in his torso. He quickly stopped the exercise. Nevertheless, the following statement and recollection came to him: "They betrayed me. They used me. When I was 18 or 20, I went to work for my father, who had always encouraged my competitiveness. It was my first real big money earning job. I was selling real estate. My father and my uncle ran the business and they promised me a lot of money and a bonus if I sold over a certain amount. I surpassed everyone's expectations. But when it came time to get the bonus, they said I wouldn't get it. But you promised," he said.

Their reply was something like: "Well, that will teach you not to trust everything people tell you."

Dan was devastated; he was in touch with his shock, his sense of betrayal and his anger. I suspect that were he able to really allow himself to fall, he might have experienced the many betrayals he had known prior to that particular incident: the realization of being used by both parents and the rage and grief underlying those experiences. But more poignantly, he might have been able to access his deep sense of emptiness and powerlessness and how manipulating others to maintain his own sense of power would be the core around which he would organize his identity.

Case Example 3

For the rigid character, falling, letting go, can mean betrayal yet again. Babette, who is a very pretty, ambitious, petite young woman of 33, has had many romantic relationships, which typically end amicably but leave her feeling once again unfulfilled and frightened that she will never find love and have a family. Recently, she has been dating a travelling musician who appears to be quite talented, handsome, cerebral and distant. She says, "He is cool." She uses the term in the current slang to mean "very good." But it is clear that she experiences him in the more common use of the word suggesting a lack of warmth, etc. Babette feels she does most of the work to keep the relationship going; she is continuously disappointed by his lack of responsiveness and emotional distance. She will write lengthy emails to which he will respond with a word or a line. She has typically avoided men whom she says are probably good for her, thoughtful, considerate, and caring.

There are two vignettes that we often refer to regarding interactions with her father who is a very self-absorbed, wealthy businessman. The first story is about his coming to New York on business and arranging to meet her for dinner. He tells her how eager he is to see her and what a great opportunity for just the two of them to get together. She is very excited to see him and is anticipating a lovely evening with her father. The day of the proposed dinner, he calls and tells her that coincidently his good friend just notified him that he too is in the city and would love to have dinner with him. He invites his daughter to join them, which she refuses. Her father is annoyed and frustrated by her response. The call over, she hung up the phone and cried. "He invites me and pushes me away. He always does shit like this."

The second story is of her visiting her parents on the west coast where this time, she has come for business. Having spent a fairly pleasant day with them and her sister, she is getting ready to go to a business event that evening. She tells the family that she will take a cab. Her father insists that it is waste of money and that he will drive her. She accepts his offer. As the time draws near to leave, Babette becomes anxious, because she is ready and her father hasn't even begun to dress. She reminds him of the time of the event and how it is getting close. He becomes agitated that she is pushing him. It ends badly, with his accusing her of being difficult. Her father is busy looking for his cuff links while the clock is ticking. Babette takes a cab to her event.

These two anecdotes speak to the experience of feeling chronically disappointed by her father and of her choosing men who fit into her characterological choreography. Her holding back is for fear of falling as she anticipates the rug being pulled out from under her yet again. "Is it any wonder," she said recently, "that I won't let myself *fall in love* with someone who will be there for me; that I don't believe it when men are kind and thoughtful; that I have to close my heart and keep testing and testing until they fail as I know they will.

3. Hang-ups and Holding Patterns

In his discussion of the chest segment, Reich (1949) originally stated that chest armor, when in an attitude of being pulled back suggests a stance of being "self-contained" or "self-controlled," of "sticking to oneself," or "being reserved." In all, these adaptations represent forms of "holding back."

Lowen saw emotional "hang-ups" as manifested in the body in such postures that he labeled the "coat-hanger type" with its raised shoulders and expression of fear; or the "meat-hook hang-up" represented by the so-called dowager's hump containing blocked anger; or the "noose" which is characteristic of the schizoid structure, among others. It seems that Lowen uses hanger types and holding patterns somewhat interchangeably, with the former being somewhat more metaphoric. Lowen (1976), Hilton (2007), and Johnson (1985; 1994) have all written about character structure, holding patterns, and accompanying falling fears. Modern bioenergetic analysts fundamentally agree that the impact of environmental forces upon the emerging human being's basic developmental needs shape the relational, psychic and somatic structures of the individual in the form of defensive body armor. In his attempt to attach to and survive in a particular familial or caretaking environment, the individual reflexively, through his involuntary muscles, inhibits/contracts his natural strivings thereby identifying with the caretakers' frustrations, inhibitions and/or aspirations. These chronic defensive postures form the basis of one's habitual ways of relating to himself and others, as well as one's affective attitudes and cognitive styles. Some classic examples of these holding postures with their accompanying falling fears are as follows:

The schizoid character is depicted as desperately trying to "hold together" against the fear of annihilation or "falling apart."

The oral character is trying to "hold-on" in the face of collapse, or the fear of "falling behind" or "falling back."

The psychopathic/narcissistic/character tries to "hold himself up" to ward off the fear of failing, or "falling down."

The masochistic character "holds-in" as a way of avoiding the bottom from "falling-out" or making a mess.

"Holding-back" is the stance taken by the rigid character for fear of "falling on his face" or "falling forward" toward a broken-heart, thus the fear of "falling in love."

Perhaps, presaging the work of Winnicott, Reich (1949) describes an acute falling anxiety that occurred in a child of three weeks. He writes:

> "It occurred when he was taken out of his bath and put on his back on the table. It was not immediately clear whether the cooling of the skin had precipitated the falling anxiety ... the child began to cry violently, pulled back his arms as if to gain support, tired to bring his head forward, showed intense anxiety in his eyes and could not be calmed down ... There was a definite contraction in the musculature of the right shoulder ... the child had pulled back both shoulders as if to gain a hold" (p. 329).

Similarly, Feldenkrais (1949) writes about the newborn's violent reaction to being "suddenly lowered, or if support is sharply withdrawn." He notes that one can observe a

> "contraction in the all the flexors and a halt of breath ... followed by crying, accelerated pulse, and general vasomotor disturbance. The similarity of reaction of a newborn infant to withdrawal of support, and that of fright or fear in the adult is remarkable. This reaction to falling is present at birth" (p. 115).

He goes on to say "And sudden, sharp lowering of a newborn infant elicits the series of reflexes which are the reaction of the body to falling," which is the basis of all anxieties in whatever form they may eventually take (p. 117–118).

Hilton (2007) added the borderline holding pattern, which he characterized as "holding-apart," splitting as a means of warding off "falling into an abyss," or "holding-still" in Johnson's words (1991). It is not clear that the borderline represents a fixed structure in the way Lowen describes such. It seems rather to be an absence of structure, a loosely held frame. Baum (1997) likens it to a vase that is made of many broken pieces without sufficient glue to bind it. Thus it is easily fragmented and takes an enormous effort to reassemble it each time it collapses. It is like humpty-dumpty trying to put himself back together again and again. Unlike the disciplined free-fall of a trapeze-artist or a trained sky diver, Baum posits that the fear is of falling in a disorganized way, without a solid sense of being able to re-organize oneself from this position. Similarly, a supervisor of mine noted: "If one is going to 'regress in the service of the ego', it's comforting to know that you have a return ticket on the train ride back."

In his presentation of "cephalic shock," his bioenergetic translation of Winnicott's "view of the dissociated mind and body," Lewis (1980) describes aspects of the false self as embodying the following:

> "cephalic bracing, a holding, holding together and holding against the shock to its ongoing being ... This often takes the form of a premature and unnatural fight against gravity (mother) which is structured into the head, neck and shoulder girdle ... as soon as it becomes capable of thinking, this ego ability becomes part of the child's automatic cephalic process for holding on for dear life" (p. III)

> "There is no piece of the head and mind within that is ever free of the burden of holding its world together ... The infant first holds onto itself for dear life, then tries to pull up and away from the parent"(p. IV).

Dan Siegel's (1999) discussion of the disorganized attachment style points out the split between trying to get away from the terrifying parent, a natural flight response from noxious stimuli, while simultaneously seeking comfort from the caretaker (another natural biological directive) who is creating the stress. This leaves the child's sense of self and attachments quite confused and split in the way Lewis describes it.

In another context, Lewis (1974) states that it is "unrealistic to expect some patients to relate to and integrate the feeling of standing on their feet for they lost too much ground in the process of growing up." Scott Baum (2007) in his treatise on the borderline structure, reiterates this view when he writes: "It is appalling, and terrifying to become aware of the irreparability of that damage." Its implication is clear: grounding can provide the basis for one's being able to hold one's self in good stead. But when there has been too much "ground" lost, it becomes very difficult, if not impossible to make up for this lost ground and thus the individual may be stuck "holding on for dear life." It is similar to a person who had been blind or deaf from birth and then sometime in adulthood gains these senses. He or she will never be able to see or hear like the person who was born hearing or sighted. It raises the question as to whether there is a critical period before the brain closes to new learning not only in seeing, hearing and language development but to intrapsychic and interpersonal development as well. To wit are stories of feral children or those who came from abusive/neglectful backgrounds and then are adopted by good enough parents. With so much ground having been lost, the transition to a place where one feels solidity connected to reality, if possible, can take a lifetime.

Although Keleman's book, *Emotional Anatomy* (1985) is sparse in its use of the words holding and/or falling, his work concerning our adaptive reactions to insult via the startle response reflect somato-psychic positions of holding. Keleman posits that the "startle reflex is the fundamental response to any stimuli that are unknown ..." The initial response is in the upper body which, in order to focus on the novel stimulus, "must grab, hold, brace. So the beginning of the startle reaction can be characterized as a state of *hold it!*" Thus the spine stiffens and the diaphragm descends opening the airways. He goes on to say that the startle response is on a continuum from assertion to defeat, from rigidity to shock. The body reacts to environmental forces by halting pulsation, creating segmentation, and/or using more layers of its self to respond to the insult. Keleman gives us what he sees as the various somatic reactions to the startle response, depending on the event, its severity and temporality. The normal response of readying the individual to investigate, challenge and straighten-up may yield to: an upright readiness to action; a rigid pulling-up and back; a closing-up and pulling in; a protruding outward; or a collapsing and falling inward. All these positions can easily be translated into postures of "holding" oneself in the presence of powerful environmental restrictions, invasions and prohibitions as is being discussed here.

In his discussion of grounding, Keleman (1994) states that

> "If we do not have plenty of touching and holding we may never be sure of ourselves emotionally, of the ground we stand on, since we cannot trust others to hold us ... People who are not held enough have a fear of falling and hold themselves stiffly away from the earth ... [nor can they] really hold their ground with others."

Similarly, John Conger (1995) writes that, "What the mother does not touch remains undeveloped and unconceptualized, so that we grow up with impoverished images of our embodied selves." He also states that we tend to compensate for the lack of grounding "by 'holding on' with watchful eyes and the musculature of our arms and shoulders, as if we were grasping the outer world for safety."

Kindlon and Thompson (2000) note that,

> "the opiate system partially governs emotional attachment by its connection to the sense of touch. In a very real way, this tactile sense not only protects from pain ... it allows us to be comforted ... All kinds of touch result in the release of these natural painkilling opiates."

Thus, when a hurt child runs to his mother, "her touch not only brings psychological reassurance and the promise of safety, but it also literally helps relieve the pain" (p. 185). In his discussion of the usefulness of touching in psychotherapy, Jourard (1968) writes "I believe the time to dispense with the touch-taboo in psychotherapy is now" (p. 65). He goes onto say "Mothering is mediated, among other ways, by cuddling and holding. I suspect the need for such mothering is never completely lost."

If the environment cannot facilitate a good enough holding environment, then the infant/child must learn to hold herself. This is done with the few internal and external resources available at the time(s) of trauma. It is in Johnson's words (2012), "An elegant solution, based on the resources possessed at the time of their creation." Depending on when the insults to the life force of the developing human being occur, we can see the beginning development of a character structure that includes a holding pattern as an adaptation to the dread of falling within a psycho-biological-relational matrix. It must also be added that the trauma is not a once-in-awhile event, but is a fairly constant experience in the development of the individual. In fact, as Tuccillo and Baum (2012) maintain, it is the relationship between the caretaker(s) and the infant/child that is the trauma. They call it "chronic relational trauma" which is the result of chronic relational abuse. The latter abuse comes from "being dominated, or defined, or manipulated or demeaned, or seduced ... by another, in an ongoing relationship so that these destructive dynamics-power dynamics-happen regularly, chronically." Masud Kahn (1995) uses a similar term, "cumulative trauma" to describe such phenomena as daily demeaning of a child or ongoing parent conflicts to which the child consistently bears witness. From a Relational Analytic perspective, Bromberg (2011) uses the term "developmental trauma" which results from "consistent nonrecognition and disconfirmation" of the infant/child as he is. Parents, he states, relating to a child as though he were "such and such and ignoring other aspects of him as if they don't exist disconfirm the existence of those aspects of the child's relational self." He is in agreement with Tuccillo and Baum, stating that the relationship between caregiver(s) and the developing child is not the *source* of trauma, but *is* the trauma (italics added). This is poignantly depicted by a fifty-year-old male patient of mine who is struggling to feel humanly connected to others. As he was describing his early childhood experience of being the totally "good and obedient child," I noticed his hand was holding on to the strap of his backpack. I pointed that out to him. He then told me of a crustacean that lived in the Mediterranean, near where he was raised, that clung to a rock during storms. And when the storm was over it would release its holding pattern and breathe a little until the next storm came. "For me," he said, "it wasn't waiting for a storm to blow over; I was living the storm on a daily basis. My family was the storm."

4. Other Psychodynamic Views on Holding and Falling

The concept and importance of a "holding environment" is by now part of every psychodynamic therapist's understanding of early attachment and its relevance to the maturational process. Winnicott (1965, 1975) writes that without the environment the infant would fall infinitely. The infant who is held is not aware of being preserved from the infinite falling. A slight failure of holding, however, brings to the infant a sensation of infinite falling. Although the concepts of a "holding environment" and "falling forever" were not to come for another thirty years, the seeds of them are noticeable in a brief article by Ferenczi (1969) concerning "Sensations of giddiness at the end of the psycho-analytic session," originally published in 1926. He writes about the patient giving himself up wholly to free association, transference and a feeling of being in a good environment. "Suddenly this illusion is destroyed by the doctor's warning that the session is ended; he suddenly becomes conscious of the actual facts; he is not 'at home' here, but a patient like any other … this is not the helpful father that stands before him. This sudden alteration of the psychic setting, the disillusionment (when one feels as 'though fallen from the clouds') may call up … a feeling as is experienced in sudden and unexpected change of posture when one is unable to adapt oneself …

to preserve one's 'equilibrium.'" This is a clear description of the need to hold as a reaction to the fear of falling. Today we might also understand that the disillusion and concomitant body reactions are not only toward the transference figure, the analyst, who is not the idealized father, but more importantly, to the original caretaker who did not provide the necessary holding for that person's secure development. But Ferenczi did not process this for himself or with the patient, even though he was one of the early analysts who was not afraid to hold or touch a patient.

In a small book of his unpublished papers, Winnicott (1987) uses the words hold, holding, held, handle, or handling, more than forty times. He states that

> "Infant care can be described in terms of holding. He notes that holding becomes more than physical as the infant develops. But that in the beginning, actual good holding and handling facilitates the maturational process, while the opposite is equally true and development is likely to be held up. The latter is reminiscent of Lowen's concept of 'hang-ups.'"

Winnicott proceeds to say that "every distortion of the infantile developmental process is accompanied by unthinkable anxiety: disintegration, falling forever, total failure of relating to objects, etc."

Falling forever is an experience of terror without end. I have borne witness to a patient who has been in touch with this fear in dreams, reveries, or expressed as fear of heights. This experience is like a game adults often play with children at the beach where four adults, each holding a corner of a beach-blanket bounces a child, who is lying on the blanket, up and down. Everyone is having a grand old time. Now imagine that you are this child being bounced up and down on that blanket, and now having been bounced up, they all take the blanket and walk away. There is no one to catch you. The image usually produces a sense of horror, dread, and fear of annihilation.

Winnicott states that when the mothering-person is unable to provide a good enough environment for her child, to provide an auxiliary ego, there is no ground upon which to build his identity; so the infant must resort to self-holding. That is, where environmental holding, which should have provided the ground upon which a solid sense of self can develop, is absent or deeply flawed, the infant/child must learn to hold himself; and must do so with the very rudimentary capacities available to an undeveloped being.

Although he does not credit Winnicott, clearly Lowen (2003) seems to be echoing his views when he writes,

> "Babies and children are not grounded in terms of the contact between their feet and the earth. They are of course, grounded in their relationship to their real mother. When that relationship is broken, the child withdraws its energy and becomes autistic; in a very young child, this is anaclitic depression."

In his autobiography (ibid.) he writes, "When a baby is born, its ground is the warm and loving body of its mother."

Winnicott's work on "unthinkable anxiety" is very much related to Sullivan's (1953) concept of "uncanny emotions." The latter derives from what Sullivan calls the personification of "not-me" which is an unconscious

> "organization of experiences with significant people that has been subjected to such intense anxiety ... that it was impossible for the then "relatively rudimentary person to make any sense of. This very intense anxiety precipitated by a sudden, intense, negative emotional reaction on the part of the significant environment has more than a little in common with a blow to the head. And this is experienced as an *uncanny* emotion: awe, dread, loathing, horror."

Although he doesn't write much about bodily sensations other than those affecting the digestive system, like diarrhea, vomiting, revulsion, etc., Sullivan does talk about "convulsions of some muscle groups" that hold the dissociated experiences and may be manifested as tics, and/or gross motor acts that are unconscious or meaningless to the person.

To summarize, Reich (1972) suggested that allowing the life force, the energy within us, to flow freely was the hallmark of physical and mental health. The cultural and familial patterns of responding to these forces create blocks to the natural flow and it is the therapist's job to help the patient open up the resistances that present in the form of body armor; the work is about freeing the flow of energy so that it can pulsate, vibrate, contract, expand, and regulate as needed. While this is a useful foundation, Lowen allowed that this was not sufficient to permit a person to feel fully embodied, empowered and loving. Modern bioenergetic analysts, (Baum et al, 2011; Hilton, 2007; Lewis, 2007; Tonella, 2008) have taken the work of these two giants and expanded it using our current knowledge of parent-child relations, attachment styles, neuro-bio-chemical brain events as well as the importance of the energy flow within and between the patient and therapist. Still, at its foundation, it is the deep conviction of the centrality of the flow of energy, and the contractions, expansions, restrictions, blockages and resistances to that flow and the interventions that challenge these blocking patterns that engage bioenergetic analysts. One such pattern is holding in the face of the dread of falling in its various manifestations. These may be seen as self-organizing responses to chronic relational trauma, which become habitual ways of relating to the world and oneself way beyond their usefulness in present time. Yet the fear of letting go of these positions means facing the terror that set them in place to begin with.

The question is often asked, "Why do we hold onto non-productive, sometimes self-destructive patterns?" Two fundamental human needs, perhaps ones that are built into our DNA, are the need for self-cohesiveness and the "need to be our parents' child," in the words of Philip Bromberg (2011). The somato-psychic, relational patterns, the holding patterns, derived in part as an attempt to stay attached and be known in the world in which we develop, become wired into our bodies and psyches. They become a known, habitual way of thinking, behaving and feeling that are deeply engraved in our neurons and in our musculature. We don't have to rediscover ourselves in relation to ourselves and the world each time we wake up in the morning. Nor do we have to endure the powerful, and potentially destabilizing, emotions that we have tucked away in our bodies. We hold on to familiar old patterns because we are afraid to fall.

Neuro-biological Interpersonal theory offers us another view of why we repeat old patterns. Siegel (1999) writes that traumatic events that occur to an infant/child before 18–24 months of age, before the hippocampus is fully developed, may get stuck in the implicit memory system. This system is comprised of bodily sensations, motoric impulses, perceptions, emotions, schemas and a priming of the system to be vigilant. If the hippocampus is not available to give the person perspective on what is now and what was then, certain triggers in the present can set off the implicit memory system, and all that implies, leaving one to experience a current event as if it were the same as happened in the past. Without hippocampus engagement there is no perspective. He adds that the hippocampus can be turned off by among others things, excessive drinking, rage, massive release of stress hormones, and traumas.

In a discussion of the oral character, Lowen (1980) writes

> "All tensions serve the function of blocking the expression of that which is too painful. It is painful to want to suck a breast when none is available, to reach out when no one is there ... By compressing their lips, setting their jaws, and constricting their throats, children can block the desire and deaden the pain of a need that will not be fulfilled. But then, [and this is the point] as adults they are similarly blocked in their ability to reach out to another person with feeling" (p. 168)

and get what they need to work through the early traumas. "The inner emptiness remains, and the person is forced to repeat the [compensatory] experience again and again" (p. 166) until such time as she is able to re-experience and express the pain and accompanying experiences of the original traumas that are now held in the body. He likens this to Freud's repetition compulsion.

Lowen (1976) posited,

> "Whatever its origins, every holding pattern represents in the present the unconscious use of the will against the natural forces of life. For every patient, falling represents surrender or giving up of his holding pattern. Anxiety associated with the fear of falling is one of the deepest in human personality."

Discussing his own insecurity, based on his own lack of grounding, Lowen (2003) notes that he always felt nervous when he stood close to the edge of a precipice.

> "Even though I tried to keep myself straight, I could never find the position of my feet that would give me the good sense of security that many other people have. The idea that I was unconsciously leaning forward did not occur to me until I worked with a patient who sat far forward in his chair when we were discussing his problem."

Lowen realized that the patient was "ahead" of himself. And he realized that he had been doing the same thing, i.e., "scanning the foreground to pick up any evidence of danger." Lowen notes that "My body was forcing me to come to terms with my willfulness and head control." Bob Lewis might say that he was too much in his head; that he was suffering from "cephalic shock," which kept him in his head and away from his body and solid grounding – leading to a chronic sense of insecurity that he was trying to compensate for by being even more in his head. Lewis (2007) writes "Lowen's odyssey is about never having come to terms sufficiently with the shock in head (cephalic shock) to find the peace of mind that eluded him." In *Fear of Life* (1980), Lowen writes about a patient who says, "If I let go of my head, bend down, I feel weak, helpless, and frightened. I have to hold myself up." Lowen goes on to say that the back of the neck is an important "holding" area in the body, and most of us have strong tensions there because we are afraid of losing control by letting go of the head. Finally, he writes, "We hold against our anger, our sadness, and our fear. We hold in our crying and our screaming. We hold back our love. We do this because we are afraid to let go, afraid to be, afraid to live."

5. Grounding, Holding, and Falling

In writing about grounding, which is a basic tenet of his work, Lowen (2003) states that the difficulty in getting grounded lies in the fact that it is more frightening to move downward than up – the former being associated with the idea of falling. To the extent that the contact between the supporting structure of the body (the legs and feet) and the ground is compromised, there is disturbance in one's relationship to self, others and reality. Again he relates this to the "falling anxiety" which he notes is manifested in dreams of falling, fear of heights, and fear of "falling in love." He goes on to say that in a safe environment, as one lets down, the first feeling is that of sadness, a "breakdown" into tears, a surrender to the affect held in the belly, a letting go of the holding pattern. The second experience that derives from first learning to be grounded, standing on one's feet, is the feeling of standing alone. And in the interval between letting go and feeling one's feet solid on the ground, one feels a sensation of falling and profound anxiety.

In this interval lies the unexpected shock that comes from experiencing a dissociated aspect of the self. When the person doesn't feel safe enough to risk getting into his feet, the holding pattern rigidifies and/or chaos ensues. The paradox being that as one feels more grounded (held), the fear of falling lessens and thus the need to rigidify the holding pattern, or falling into chaos, is reduced. Mayer (1996) writes

> "We have to give up one thing in order to see the other. We have to lose what's familiar in order to see what's new ... Giving up our habitual grounding in rational thought to see something else, even just for a moment-that's anything but easy for most of us" (p. 138).

Providing a safe and grounded environment comes in many varieties. One may hold with one's eyes, one's voice, one's words, one's physical being, attitude, and so forth. Anita Madden (2005) writes that "holding and support of the head creates a form of grounding. Such as is supplied by a 'good enough' mother." In a discussion of her own experience as she was detoxifying her body, Madden describes the shock her body was in and how she clenched to avoid the cold/shivering she felt; she was afraid that if she "let go" to the shivering, she might die. "I wanted to hold on. I wanted to let go." Note the paradox again.

At another time in her life, after having lived for over a year with great stress, she describes a workshop- experience with Peter Fernald, who having created a safe enough environment encouraged her to stand in a grounding position. She states that, "As vibrations increased throughout my body, I felt I could no longer stand up. I could no longer 'hold up, or 'hold on' … I lay down on a mattress … I felt relaxed, open and re-energized. I had let go." Anita is describing an experience in which she risked falling, and having falling safely she was able to let go of the defensive vigilance that had gripped her the past year. She was for that moment grounded in reality.

Danita Hall's (2013) presentation on grounding speaks to the importance of grounding in bioenergetic work, its origins, manifestations, and connections to developmental and relational processes. Using the Bow Position as a basic grounding exercise, she points to the limits of the various characterological structures to experiencing a full body experience. In this context, she reiterates Lewis's (1974) caveat that it is …" unrealistic to expect some patients to relate to and integrate the feeling of standing on their feet for they have lost too much ground in the process of growing up."

Describing various examples, using different grounding techniques, Hall points out that attention must be paid by the therapist to the developmental and characterological structure of the patient. Again underscoring the importance of relationship in grounding, she states, "Not only does grounding come from being held and supported by the ground, the therapist's touch and holding and focusing words act as a ground …"

A patient of mine, who had recently been diagnosed with a chronic illness, was experiencing the world as though the ground had fallen out beneath him. As I was compassionately bearing witness to his terror, despair and confusion, I asked him if he wanted me to hold him. "It wasn't necessary," he replied. "I feel you holding me with your voice."

It is clear that the concept of grounding has evolved, as has the practice of bioenergetic therapy which more and more is taking into account the importance of the therapeutic relationship and the space within which that evolves; but also the concepts of attachment, holding and falling which are part of that matrix have evolved as central issues in the relational and characterological development of the individual. As Scott Baum (2007) has written, "The therapeutic relationship acts as a holding environment for the truth to emerge."

6. English Language Expressions of Holding and Fear of Falling

Table 2 presents a list of English language expressions having to do with the fear of falling related to character structure and holding patterns. There are other expressions in the English language that have not been included in the table below, but which may fit into the suggested paradigm presented, such as "falling off the wagon," "falling asleep," or "falling on hard times" for example.

One more disclaimer: I am not sure how the idiomatic expressions that follow translate into other languages. I assume there are equivalent expressions that carry similar meanings but I cannot be certain. With this caveat in mind, what follows are lists of holding patterns (somatic adaptations), corresponding expressions of fear of falling (intra-psychic) and common expressions (holding attitudes) depicting attitudes or postures toward others (interpersonal). There are many expressions that incorporate the words *holding* or *falling* that have specific meanings in the English language. Adding to the bioenergetic theorizing already cited on holding and falling, I have expanded on Hilton's (2007) interpersonal stances (holding attitudes) and clustered them under the rubric of each of the classical character structures subscribed to by most bioenergetic analysts. As no character structure presents in pure form, there is clearly overlap of postures, fears and attitudes presented. I have included the so-called borderline structure because Hilton (2007) and Johnson (1991) have written about it as a holding pattern. But, I do so hesitantly because of the controversial nature of the concept at this time; nor am I sure, as stated before, that it is a character structure, armor, in the way envisioned by Lowen. Rather as suggested earlier, it may be a different order of structure or lack thereof. It may make more sense to view it on a continuum that runs from psychotic ... borderline ... neurotic ... personality disorder ... to character style. Johnson (1994) has written on this issue, as has Schroeter (2009). She states that "I have contemplated that borderline is not even a character type ... a person may be any character type, but within that type, operate at a lower ... to middle ... to higher level of functioning." Struggling with the concept of borderline, Rentoul (2010) states, "It is not obvious what it is the borderline of: whether of health, of sexuality, of psychosis, or, as I believe, of being able to exist at all." He speaks of the baby's having to hang on because of being driven to the edge of endurance. Noting that these views are not dealt with well within psychoanalysis, he writes, "though fear of falling might have some relationship to it" (p. 61).

The confusion with the borderline concept may be the result of two axes emanating from different roots. Lowen's classical character structures sits on Freudian/Reichian libido theory which emphasizes pleasure-seeking as the primary motivation of human existence; whereas consideration of a continuum from psychotic through borderline through character style derives primarily from the Object Relations/Self Psychology schools of thought which posit a libido that is object-seeking. And although Lowen in his early writing occasionally

Psychological Organization	Grounding
Psychotic	No ground
Borderline	Shifting ground
Neurotic	Shaky ground
Character Disorder	Contracted ground
Character Style	More Solid ground

Table 1. Psyche-soma matrix

touches upon the importance of early interpersonal interaction in the formation of character, because he too is deeply influenced by the Freudian/Reichian pleasure-seeking libido, it is not until the latter schools, primarily derived from Object Relations Psychology, that we come to understand the importance of early attachment and caregiver-child interaction as formative of self-structure and relationship with others, or lack thereof. The latter perhaps relating more to the axis from psychotic to character style suggested above. It may be that character structure is essentially a means by which the individual has developed armor in order to hold onto, contain and protect whatever rudiments of an energetic vital self still exist after having been thwarted by opposing environmental forces; while Self-Psychology and Object-Relations theories may be explanatory of ways in which we see ourselves in relation to self and/or another as we seek to connect to other subjective selves. Thus one may regard the object-seeking self in a complex interaction with an energetic vitality-seeking self that is armored to protect it from future trauma. Perhaps Lowen (2003) saw this in his 90s, when as he returned to his concepts of grounding and hang-ups, reiterated that people who do not have their feet on the ground are hung-up; to which he added that "The state of being hung-up is a psychological condition, whereas not being grounded is a physical state." These conditions complement each other, because they are really two aspects of the same state of not being fully connected to the reality of one's being. He goes on to say that "Bioenergetics uses dual approaches – a physical approach and a psychological approach" (p. 143). He likens this to having two legs to walk on.

Another bioenergetic way of viewing the two-legged approach to our understanding of the psyche-soma matrix may be accomplished by juxtaposing the concepts of grounding and psychological organization; again emphasizing the importance of grounding and its relationship to reality as seen in table 1.

What is also being posited here, in table 2 and what follows is that the two-legged approach postulated by Lowen, can only work in a safe and holding interpersonal set of arms. Having two legs to stand on does not mean a person is able to move about gracefully, securely and with dignity in the world. Our two legs, physically and intra-psychically operate within an interpersonal world. What is clear is that we are born into, develop and can change only in the context of an interpersonal matrix. Energy flows and can be blocked not only within the individual but also between the individual and another or many others. So to think of the body alone or the psyche alone or even as a duality is to miss the point that these are but parts of a tripartite system involving the energetic and informational flow within as well as between people. Herein we have been discussing the informational/energetic flow between the infant/child and her primary caretaker(s). This energetic/informational flow gets stored in the psyche-soma and forms the basis of whether the developing human will have a secure, insecure or disorganized attachment style which seems to be so much a part of one's character structure and transferential interactions with others.

Schizoid Structure		
Holding Patterns (Somatic)	**Fear of (Intra-psychic)**	**Holding Attitudes (Interpersonal)**
Holding Together	Falling Forever	Holding Off
	Falling Off a Cliff	Holding at a Distance
	Falling Away	Holding at Bay
	Falling Through Space	
	Falling Apart	

Oral Structure		
Holding Patterns (Somatic)	**Fear of (Intra-psychic)**	**Holding Attitudes (Interpersonal)**
Holding On	Falling Into	Holding Court
	Falling Back	Holding Accountable
	Falling Behind	Holding Aside

Psychopathic/Narcissistic Structure		
Holding Patterns (Somatic)	**Fear of (Intra-psychic)**	**Holding Attitudes (Interpersonal)**
Holding Up	Falling Down	Holding Court
	Falling on his Ass/Face	Holding in Contempt
	Falling from Great Heights	Holding Forth

	Falling Short	Holding One's Head Up
	Falling from Grace	
	Falling For	
	Falling out of Favor	
Masochistic Structure		
Holding Patterns (Somatic)	**Fear of (Intra-psychic)**	**Holding Attitudes (Inter-personal)**
Holding In	Falling Out	Holding Hostage
	Falling Under	Holding Out
	Falling from Grace	Holding To
		Holding Down
Rigid Structure		
Holding Patterns (Somatic)	**Fear of (Intra-psychic)**	**Holding Attitudes (Inter-personal)**
Holding Back	Falling on his Face	Holding Against
	Falling Forward	Holding his Horses
	Falling in Love	Holding Firm
	Falling For	Holding Tight
	Falling to Earth	Holding Court
Borderline Structure		
Holding Patterns (Somatic)	**Fear of (Intra-psychic)**	**HoldingAttitudes (Inter-personal)**
Holding Apart	Falling Into an Abyss	Holding Around
Holding Still	Falling Forever	Holding Aside
	Falling Through	Holding in Contempt

Table 2. Character structures, holding patterns, fears of falling and holding attitudes

7. Providing the Holding/Grounding Needed to Facilitate Falling

The best-known falling exercise in the bioenergetic quiver of techniques is Lowen's (1976). Assuring there is a soft place on which to land, he has the patient put all her weight on one leg, bending the knee fully, the other foot being used for balance only. Now the person is directed to stand in that position until she falls. It is important that the person not let herself fall consciously; it should be involuntary. It is an anxiety-provoking situation, he says, because most people are afraid of losing control of their bodies. Lowen also suggests the person breathe easily and keep saying, "I am going to fall." The therapist, when appropriate, asks what falling means to the patient. The exercise is repeated several times. Ultimately, the person may realize that falling is not the end. The body gets up again. In fact, falling to earth may allow a renewal of energy in the awareness of being grounded. But when the ground, the caretaker, is not a source of holding/grounding, there is an understandable fear of falling to mother earth that isn't there or is there in a highly anxious and/or disorganized manner.

It seems that such an exercise derived, as most of his exercises, from Lowen's (2003) attempt to get more into his own body; a struggle he apparently worked on his whole life. The exercise described above may be more appropriate for the rigid character structure. Although, I have used it effectively with people having pre-oedipal character structures. It is also seems useful for very experienced patients, no matter the character structure, as is demonstrated by Anita Madden's description of her experience with Fernald that was mentioned earlier. But for people struggling with pre-Oedipal issues, the charge may be far more than is containable. Pat Ogden, et al (2006) point out the importance of holding safely. What does that mean to hold safely? It means, as Hall (2013) has written, to be cognizant of the developmental and characterological structure of the person with whom you are working. To be aware of the amount of charge that is manageable. To provide a holding environment that respects the individual. It means, in bioenergetic terms, to provide an atmosphere in which grounding, which may come in the forms of specific exercises, touching, the relationship between the therapist and the patient, etc., may begin to be embodied within the context of a safe environment that facilitates taking a risk of letting go and falling.

John Conger (1995) provides a seven-stage developmental schema for grounding from initially grounding on the mother's belly to standing up straight to ultimately being grounded to Nature and perhaps, as Baum (2007) put it, to being connected to the benevolence of the Universe. Adding to the concept of grounding as relational, Danita Hall (2013) states that, "Grounding is formed through contact: contact as a person-to-person connection in which the being and reality of the other is experienced and recognized." Quoting Lowen, who says that the more one feels grounded, the more charge and feeling one can handle, she goes on to note that grounding is a process that facilitates expansion. As an example of finding a grounding exercise that fits, she describes a young man with a schizoid structure for whom standing up compelled him to "lock his knees, or stiffen his arms and shoulders, to avoid fragmentation. Having him move to a lying down position, with knees up and feet on the mat, took some of the pressure off his joints, but the regressive pull became intolerable and he stiffened up." Finally she had him sit on a large gym ball while pressing his feet and gently moving up and down. This seemed to allow for the expression of expansion. In this way, Hall points out the relational nature of grounding. She writes that

> "Not only does grounding come from being held and supported by the ground, the therapist's touch and holding and focusing words act as a ground. It was her being attuned to him and shifting her interventions accordingly that provided grounding for a man whose family did not allow for any expression of vulnerability or emotional exploration."

Keleman (1975) writes that containing and expressing energy allows us to be connected to the earth and expand into the social world. These are elements of grounding. We see here again that grounding has a personal and interpersonal aspect. He goes on to say that "Interference with one's rooting and expanding is manifested in how one relates to the earth, reflected as poor bodily form, and in how one relates to one's social surround, reflected as misshapen connections with others." This may be seen as personal character structure and the interpersonal holding attitudes being discussed here. Keleman points out that "encouraged to develop groundedness," depth of feeling and imagination can grow from which we can further ground our lives.

The are many well documented grounding exercises (Lowen, 1976, 1977; Conger, 1994; Hilton, 2007; Schroeter & Thomson, 2011); but not so many falling exercises. It is the contention here that a certain amount of grounding/holding is necessary for the patient to feel safe enough to let himself fall. There is the classic falling exercise by Lowen, described earlier. For many people who are too much in their heads and cannot "allow their body, including their head, to collapse under them …" Lewis (1986) recommends

> "directly involving the head by having the patient rotate his head while knees are bent, there is immediately much less cerebral control, and the stimulation to the vestibular apparatus produces sensations of loss of equilibrium and falling, which are exactly what most people who are 'in their heads' guard against by keeping their heads relatively immobile."

This has certainly been my experience. It wasn't until I could "unorganizeunorganized" my head/neck/shoulder girdle control by rotating my head during the classic falling exercise that I could let myself fall. In an earlier paper, Lewis (1976) proposes that dissonance between the child and the caregiver is the basis

> "of falling anxiety and premature ego development, or what we in Bioenergetics call the inability to get out of one's head – an attribute that seems to cut across all character structures. It is this dissonance, and the resultant falling anxiety and premature ego development, *structured into our bodies*, that prevent the quality of grounding we strive for in Bioenergetics" (ibid., p. VI).

For patients with pre-oedipal structures and less firm grounding, utilizing the falling fears listed in table 2., the therapist might begin by having the patient sit with his feet feeling rooted to the ground and asking him to imagine what would happen if for example he were to fall off a cliff, fall behind, or fall out of favor and so forth. What does it mean? How does it feel? Where is it felt in the body? What sensations are experienced? What does it make him feel like doing? What images or memories come to mind? How does that experience impact his relationship to self and others? What is the therapist feeling as the patient goes through these exercises?

Case Example 4

A 35 year-old male patient of mine, who was struggling with changing careers and feeling quite uncertain about his future, noted that he felt ungrounded going forward. I knew that his parents had divorced when he was three years old, and they fought over custody of their only child in a way that terrified him. He learned to keep quiet and say nothing about what he felt or wanted because he was sure that they would use whatever he told one parent as ammunition against the other in their custody battle. When he stood up to begin a grounding exercise that I thought might be a starting place for developing his ability to move forward, I noted that his feet, which were at least a size 12, befitting his well over 6 foot stature, were in a splayed position, like a ballet dancer in third position. I asked him if he could put his feet parallel to each other. As he began to do this, he stopped abruptly and said that he couldn't; he was afraid that he would fall if he took his feet out of that position and unlocked his knees. I asked him to imagine what would happen if he were to fall. "There would be nobody there to catch me, he replied. And it would upset my sense of balance." Locked in that position made it very difficult for him to move forward. It was as though he had one foot pointed in his father's direction and the other toward his mother. He was keeping a delicate balance in order to maintain a connection with each parent and also, he thought, not giving them fodder for their quarrels. It rendered him unable to move forward and feel grounded in his own direction.

From an interpersonal perspective, the therapist might have the patient exaggerate his stance, (in the style of Keleman's (1987) HOW exercises) of holding off, holding court, or holding in contempt, etc., and then inquire into those experiences as suggested above. I might have asked the same patient to exaggerate his splayed stance of holding at bay or holding apart which may have yielded other avenues of inquiry: perhaps regarding the splitting that Siegel (1999) talks about in his discussion of disorganized attachment or Johnson's (1991) suggestion of holding still as an adaptive device to ward off falling forever. In Hilton's (2007) discussion of character development there are a series of dyadic (mother-child) exercises that may be used to demonstrate how character-related falling fears and holding patterns are manifested interpersonally.

Although Hall (2013) doesn't mention falling per se, she echoes the theme of many of the theorists quoted and the central point of this paper, when she writes that "A leap of faith is involved in the formation of new ground – for there is an entering into the unknown – a step into experience that is shared and contained by the therapeutic holding environment offering a new experience of the present – a new grounding." And I would add, a setting in which it is safe to fall and explore the holding patterns that were needed to maintain attachments to significant others and to keep whatever remains of the self intact.

8. Summary

Much of the writing and theorizing in the psychodynamic literature about falling has been about very early trauma as in the fear of falling forever. And the suggestion has been offered that some may never recover the ground lost. It is this author's contention that although all character structures may not involve a fear of falling forever per se, (nor am I sure of that) there resides in each character structure a holding pattern, a fear of letting go, that is related to a fear of falling *characteristic* of that structure which can be seen in the body and concomitantly intra-psychically and interpersonally. It is also understood that these holding patterns serve to protect whatever part of self is alive and still trying to develop.

So that even for those individuals who have been severely traumatized early and continuously in life, there is a possibility of developing some form of grounding, in a safe environment, that will allow the person to let go a little, fall a little, and develop to a place where he or she can pulsate, contract and expand as much as they are able, in order to have a life experience that is more embodied, authentic and grounded than before they embarked on the journey toward healing and authenticity.

Maybe you're going to fall.
But it is better than not starting at all.
(From *Everybody Says Don't*
Stephen Sondheim, 1964)

References

Baum, S. (1997). Living on shifting sands: grounding and borderline personality organization. *Journal of Contemporary Psychoanalysis, 27*(1), 61–86.

Baum, S. (2007). Living on purpose: reality, unreality and the life of the body. *Bioenergetic Analysis*, (17), 165–188.

Baum, S. (2011) in collaboration with Guze, V., Hall, D., Madden, A. Panvini, R., Rhoads, E., Schneider, J., Silberstein, J., Tucillo, E. *Modern bioenergetics: an integrative approach to psychotherapy*. New York: Society for Bioenergetic Analysis.

Bromberg, P.M. (2011). *The shadow of the tsunami and the growth of the relational mind*. New York: Rutledge.

Conger, J.P. (1995). *The body in recovery: somatic psychotherapy and the self*. Berkeley, CA: Frog Books.

Feldenkrais, M. (1949). *Body & mature behavior: a study of anxiety, sex, gravitation, & learning*. Berkeley, CA: Frog Books.

Ferenczi, S. (1969). *Further contributions to the theory and technique of psychoanalysis*. London: The Hogarth Press.

Hall, D. (2013). *Grounding: a developmental and relational process*. Presentation, IIBA. Palermo, Italy.

Hilton, R. (2008). *Relational somatic psychotherapy*. M. Sieck (Ed.). Santa Barbara, CA: Santa Barbara Graduate Institute.

Johnson, S.M. (1985). *Characterological transformation: the hard work miracle*. New York: Norton.

Johnson, S.M. (1987). *Humanizing the narcissistic style*. New York: Norton.

Johnson, S.M. (1991). *The symbiotic character*. New York: Norton.

Johnson, S.M. (1994). *Character styles*. New York: Norton.

Johnson, S.M. (2012). *Stars in stone: a clinician's guide to masochism*. http://www.stephenjohnsonphd.comm/?id=books.

Jourard, S.M. (1968). *Disclosing man to himself*. New York: Van Nostrand Co.

Kahn, M. (1995). The concept of cumulative trauma. *Journal of the American Academy of Child and Adolescent Psychiatry, 34*, 541–565.

Keleman, S. (1975). *The human ground: sexuality, self and survival*. Berkley, CA: Center Press.
Keleman, S. (1985). *Emotional anatomy*. Berkley, CA: Center Press.
Keleman, S. (1987). *Embodying experience: forming a personal life*. Berkley, CA: Center Press.
Kindlon, D. and Thompson, M. (2000). *Raising Cain: protecting the emotional life of boys*. New York: Ballantine Books.
Lewis, R.A. (1974). A developmental view of bioenergetic therapy. *Energy and Character, 5*, 41–47.
Lewis, R.A. (1976). The psychosomatic basis of premature ego development. *The Training Manual*. New York: Institute for Bioenergetic Analysis.
Lewis, R.A. (1984). Cephalic shock as a somatic link to the false self personality. *Comprehensive Psychotherapy, 4*, 101–114.
Lewis, R.A. (1986). Getting the head to really sit on one's shoulder: a first step in grounding the false self. *Bioenergetic Analysis*, (2), 56–77.
Lewis, R.A. (2007). Bioenergetics in search of a secure self. *Bioenergetic Analysis*, (17), 135–163.
Lowen, A. (1976). *Bioenergetics: the revolutionary therapy that uses the language of the body to heal the problems of the mind*. New York: Penquin Books.
Lowen, A. (1977). *The way to vibrant health: a manual of bioenergetic exercises*. Alachua, FL: Bioenergetic Press.
Lowen, A. (1980). *Fear of Life*. Hinesburg, VT: The Alexander Lowen Foundation.
Lowen, A. (1983). *Narcissism: denial of the true self*. New York: Macmillan Publishing Co.
Lowen, A. (2003). *Honoring the body: an autobiography*. Hinesburg, VT: The Alexander Lowen Foundation.
Madden, A. (2005). *The orgastic reflex*. Presentation. The Professional Development Workshop. West Cornwall, CT: IIBA.
Mayer, E.L. (1996). Subjectivity and intersubjectivelity of clinical facts. *International Journal of Psychoanalysis, 77*, 709–737.
Ogden, P., Minton, K., and Pain, C. (2006). *Trauma and the body: a sensorimotor approach to psychotherapy*. New York: Norton.
Reich, W. (1949). *The cancer biopathy*. New York: The Orgone Institute Press.
Reich, W. (1949). *Character analysis*. New York: Touchstone.
Rentoul, R.W. (2010). *Ferenczi's language of tenderness*. New York: Jason Aronson.
Schroeter, V. (2009). Borderline character structure revisited. *Bioenergetic Analysis*, (19), 31–51.
Schroeter, V. and Thomson, B. (2011). *Bend into shape: techniques for bioenergetic therapists*. Self-Published. Encinitas, CA: Schroeter and Thomson.
Siegel, D. (1999). *The developing mind*. NY: Guilford Press.
Sullivan, H.S. (1953). *The interpersonal theory of psychiatry*. New York: Norton.
Tonella, G. (2008). Paradigms for bioenergetic analysis at the dawn of the 21st century. *Bioenergetic Analysis*, (18), 27–59.
Tuccillo, E. and Baum, S. (2012). *Chronic relational trauma and the origin of borderline personality organization*. Presentation. IIBA. Brazil.
Winnicott, D.W. (1965). *The maturational processes and the facilitating environment*. New York: International University Press.
Winnicott, D.W. (1975). *Through pediatrics to psychoanalysis*. New York: Basic Books.
Winnicott, D.W. (1987). *Babies and their mothers*. New York: Addison-Wesley Publishing Co.
Wolf, F.A. (1989). *Taking the quantum leap: the new physics for non-scientists*. New York: Harper & Row.

Acknowledgement

This article would not be in its present version were it not for the very careful and thoughtful input from Dr. Scott Baum to whom the author is very grateful. Thanks also to Dr. Robert Lewis for his input and encouragement and for helping me see how important it is to consider the head a vital part of the body.

About the Author

Dr. Perlman is a clinical psychologist and psychoanalyst in private practice in New York City. He is a former Director of Internship Training at Manhattan Psychiatric Center and is in his fourth year of training with the New York Society of Bioenergetic Analysis.

Gerald Perlman, PhD
41 Park Avenue, Ste. 1D
New York, NY 10016
USA
E-mail: geraldperlmanphd@gmail.com

Elements of Comprehending Change-Processes in BA[1]

From Isolated Self-Regulation to Interactive Regulation: Embodied Resonance (Empathy) and Physical Encounter

Joerg Clauer

Abstracts

English

On behalf of two case studies this paper aims to present some elements in comprehending change-processes of patients suffering from severe disorders. Knowledge of infant research and neurobiology are used as a blueprint for that. Healing processes are considered to take place on the level of implicit embodied relational knowledge – and embodied resonance (empathy), physical cooperation and rhythms to be fundamental elements. Spatiotemporal, affective and bodily proprioceptive forms of communicative exchange – and less *the* psychodynamic content – are of fundamental importance to self-development of patients in this perspective.

Key words: embodied resonance, fragmented self-experience, mutual developmental process, physical cooperation, "primary triangle"

German

Dieser Artikel versucht anhand zweier Fallgeschichten einige Wirkfaktoren zu identifizieren, die uns helfen können, Veränderungsprozesse bei Patienten mit

1 Extended version of a lecture that was held at the 1st Maschsee Symposium in Hanover, Germany in June 2014 and was tied to a co-lecture by Franz Herberth. I thank the Maschsee

schweren Störungen/Erkrankungen besser zu verstehen. Dazu werden Erkenntnisse aus der Säuglingsforschung und Neurobiologie herangezogen. Heilungsprozesse würden demzufolge auf der Ebene des implizit-körperlichen Beziehungswissens angestoßen – und Empathie als verkörperter Resonanzprozess sowie körperliche Kooperation und Rhythmen wären fundamentale Bausteine dieser Prozesse. Aus dieser Perspektive betrachtet ist es weniger der psychodynamische Inhalt, der von grundlegender Bedeutung für die Selbstentwicklung von Patienten ist, als vielmehr räumliche, zeitliche, affektive und propriozeptiv-körperliche Formen der Kommunikation.

French

Cet article expose deux situations cliniques dans le but de mieux comprendre les éléments favorables au changement pour les patients qui souffrent de problématiques sévères. Ce sont les connaissances issues des recherches infantiles et de la neurobiologie qui en sont la base. On considère que les capacités relationnelles implicites et somatiques sont au cœur du processus de guérison; la résonnance corporelle (l'empathie), la coopération physique et la rythmicité en sont des composants fondamentaux. Dans cette perspective, pour le développement au niveau du Soi, plus que le contenu psychodynamique, ces sont les interactions et communications spatiotemporelles, affectives et proprioceptives qui seront déterminantes.

Spanish

Por medio de dos estudios de casos, este ensayo tiene como objetivo presentar algunos elementos para entender los procesos de cambio en pacientes que sufren de trastornos graves. Los conocimiento acerca de las investigaciones infantiles y neurobiología se utilizan como un anteproyecto para el mismo. Se considera que los procesos de curación ocurren a un nivel de conocimiento implícito incorporado relacional y de resonancia incorporada (empatía); la cooperación física y los ritmos también son elementos fundamentales. Las *formas* de intercambio comunicativo espaciotemporal, afectivo y corporal propioceptivo – *y menos del contenido psicodinámico* – son de fundamental importancia para el desarrollo individual de los pacientes en esta perspectiva.

Working Group whose work and discussions are a constant source of rich suggestions. I am particularly grateful to my colleague Franz Herberth for his vital, cooperative-stimulating and respectful cooperation.

Portuguese

Tendo por base dois estudos de caso, este artigo visa mostrar alguns elementos para a compreensão dos processos de mudança em pacientes que sofrem de desordens severas. Para isso, utilizamos o conhecimento de pesquisas sobre bebês e da neurobiologia. Considera-se que os processos de cura ocorrem ao nível do conhecimento relacional incorporado implícito, sendo que a ressonância incorporada (empatia), a cooperação física e o ritmo são elementos fundamentais. Formas proprioceptivas corporais, espaço-temporais e afetivas de troca comunicativa são de importância crucial (maior que o conteúdo psicodinâmico) para o auto-desenvolvimento dos pacientes em questão.

1. Introduction

Lowen (1986) described the treatment of psychosomatic illnesses as a difficult task, especially inflammatory diseases of the digestive tract. In 2007, I made some observations in this journal regarding the treatment process of these disorders based on a successful bioenergetic analysis of a patient with ulcerative colitis. In doing so, I not only emphasized the intense transference/counter-transference process but also the particular importance of the three s's: slowness, safety and support.

This paper now attempts to continue to examine the active processes and facilitating elements of change processes during Bioenergetic long-term treatments. It presents reflections on the relevance of empathy (embodied resonance) and bodily cooperation in the therapeutic process of patients with "early disorders." "Early disorders" are not only disorders of vitality affects or vitality dynamics (cf. Stern, 1986/2011) but primarily self-loss experiences or fragmentations, i. e. the loss of the cohesion of self-experience. Orange, Atwood and Stolorow (1997, p. 47f.) have differentiated the following self-loss experiences:

- Psychic fragmentation: the experience of psychological selfhood disintegrates into parts
- Somatic fragmentation: the unity and integrity of the experience of your body is lost
- Psychosomatic fragmentation: your body and mind are experienced as irrevocably separated.

In the case studies two patients tried to preserve their own threatened self in various ways:

- ➢ A patient with a psychosomatic fragmentation and his desperate attempt to control his surroundings as much as possible for the safety of his own self-experience.
- ➢ A second patient suffered from mental and somatic fragmentations with disturbances to her basal vitality dynamics combined with a helpless, resignative abandonment of her self-assertion.

Sander (2009, p. 163) said that self-psychology must turn to two areas in order to understand the ontogenesis of behavior and psychological organization: early childhood development and biology (that is today neurobiology too). This also corresponds to the understanding of bioenergetic body psychotherapy.

The present IIBA-website uses in explaining Bioenergetic Analysis a statement of Robert Lewis about body and words: "we listen to the inner resonance – of your inchoate secrets – as it lives in your body … but we also listen carefully to your words and are touched by them when they come from a depth no one can put a hand on." Lewis (2000, 2004, 2005) himself like Resneck-Sannes (2002, 2012) and many others have presented case stories and attempts to understand the importance of attunement and resonance or bodily interaction as elements for change processes in Bioenergetic analysis and psychotherapies. In even more detail the "Boston Change Process Study Group" for about two decades already is occupied with investigating change processes in psychotherapies (Stern et al., 2010). They have a background of psychoanalysis and infant research with a paradigm of research that focuses on the attunement in the mother-infant-dyad mainly via exteroceptive channels i.e. vision and hearing. This misses mostly a focus that is important for Bioenergetic Analysis, a more systemic point of view that integrates the father (Fivaz-Depeursinge & Carboz-Warnery, 2001) and the bodily sensorial channels of touch, proprioception and tactile sensations.

This paper tries to integrate some of those points of view in understanding change processes in the presented cases of Bioenergetic therapies. Special attention is thereby paid to embodied resonance (empathy) and bodily cooperation in the therapeutic relational dialogue which is considered as a mutual developmental process within the patient-therapist dyad. Before I describe the cases, I will first direct my attention to early childhood development and (neuro-)biology in order to create a framework for the comprehension and comments on the case histories.

2. Early Childhood Development

2.1. Empathy and Dyadic Affect Attunement

Empathy is the basis for attunement processes between the infant and mother or other caregivers at the beginning of life already and, therefore, also for the beneficial self-development of the baby (cf. Schwaber, 2013, p. 98). Sander understood the coordinated interaction between mother and infant as a *resonance between two systems* (cited by Schore, 2005, p. 403). Winnicott (1974) had already pointed out that the mother and infant only exist as a system, and that there is no baby without the mother and vice versa. Both are dependent on each other in their biological regulation. One example is breastfeeding. It is of vital importance to the diet of the infant and can be vital to the mother after childbirth since it helps her uterus to regress and can counteract bleeding and infection. Otherwise, the self-regulatory skills of the mother could be overwhelmed and she would have to depend on medical assistance.

This interdependence is obviously significantly greater for the baby. Its immature system needs the regulating aids of the mother, particularly after birth, not only in order to survive and to maintain physical homeostasis, but also to stimulate the baby and to regulate and dampen any stress states and over-excitation. In terms of its sleep-wake rhythms and instable vegetative regulation of its temperature for example, the infant is largely dependent on the empathetic, contingent regulatory care of a caregiver. This is made easier by a – hormonally mediated – particularly pronounced empathy of the mother towards *her* infant (cf. Ammaniti & Trentini, 2009). According to Stern (1992), all these processes can be assigned to the phase of the emerging sense of self. The infant does not internalize the object or partial objects, but rather *the process of mutual regulation* (Stern et al., 2012).

Sander (2009) not only described important organizing principles for these somatopsychic attunement processes like the principle of specificity, but in particular the principle of rhythmicity and the agency of the individual. Moreover, he formulated the following phases of problems in the development of the mother-infant system (month of life = ML):

1. Primary regulation of biological processes (for homeostasis)	1st–3rd ML
2. Reciprocally coordinated exchange of physical activities	4th–6th ML
3. Initiative of child's activities	7th–9th ML
4. Focus on the availability and limits of the mother	10th–13th ML

5. Self-assertion in opposition to the mother 14th–20th ML
6. Recognition (awareness, expression+ regard of intentions) 18th–36th ML
7. Continuity (recognition +cohesion of a differentiated self) 18th–36th ML

I also mention Stern's developmental stages of a sense of self here. Important to me are the evolving and prevailing forms of "*NO*" in these phases of a sense of self, which I will employ together with Sander's phases, to comment on these case histories. They are a central part in the development of the infant's emancipation just as much as the development of patients with disorders in their self-experience and are summarized in figure 1.

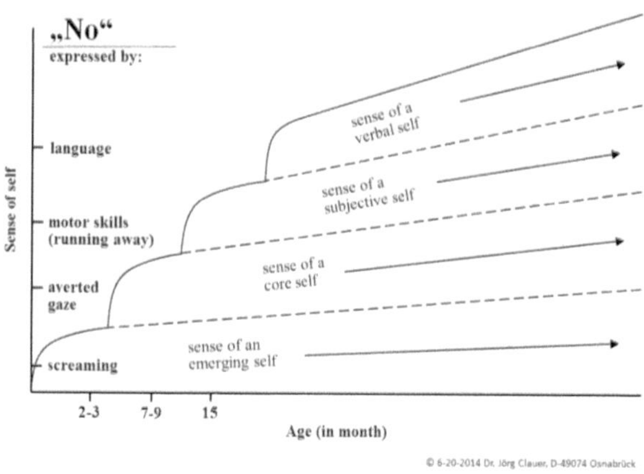

Figure 1. Developmental phases of the sense of self and delimitation, of saying "NO" (according to Stern, 1986)

In vitally important process of breastfeeding we already can observe two essential interactive regulatory processes within the dyad. One channel of communication was frequently more the focus of the attention of researchers. It primarily involves eye contact, facial expressions and the exchange of affects, e. g. during playful moments after breastfeeding. The second channel of *bodily-cooperative attunement is a separate dynamic developmental trajectory* that receives a great deal of attention in body psychotherapies and that also includes contact and skin contact. For a long time, this second area received little attention in the research on the mother-child dyad (however, see e. g. Beebe et al., 2010, 2014).

2.2. From the Dyad to the Triad: Cooperation and Physical Principles of Organization

Triangulation has particular status in the theory and thinking of psychoanalysis and its resulting methods such as bioenergetic analysis. In practice, however, analytical psychotherapy, including self-psychological methods and BA, were primarily concerned with disorders of affective exchange, bonding and mentalization processes. Neurobiology and infant research had likewise focused on affect attunement for a long time. At least from a physical standpoint, all these perspectives primarily deal with processes within a rather distanced *dyad*.

It was only the systemic perspective inspired research on the "primary triangle" – the playful interaction of infant, mother *and* father – by Fivaz-Depeursinge and Carboz-Warnery (2001), Fivaz-Depeursinge and colleagues (2010) and by von Klitzing (2002) for example, that shifted bodily attunement processes more into the focus of infant research. It shows how, starting from birth, family cooperation by the parents promotes infant development. The infant is actively seeking joint/triadic communication. So-called family alliances, i.e. cooperation in the family, require the *involvement* of all three members. This involvement and relational attunement can, as in the dyad, become easily disturbed. If the *parents' ability to cooperate is disturbed, then the triad disintegrates into dyads or monads.* Restoring (or securing) this cooperation is, according to the research, dependent on certain physical organizational patterns between the three family members (cf. Clauer, 2009a, 2011, 2013a,b,c). This was already evident in the developmental stage of the body-core self (in two to three-month-old infants) and is based on four physical interaction levels, which are linked to corresponding mental functions:

1. Pelvis = *participation*: the *orientation of the lower body* towards one another is fundamental and crucial as to whether or not all three partners in the relationship are involved in the interplay (basal rootedness of social interactions, *turns towards* the partner).
2. Torsos = *organization*: the relation of the upper body (shoulders) indicates whether or not each partner is aware of his/her role (*leans towards* the partner at the appropriate distance).
3. Gazes = *focus of attention*: the position of the head (direction of gaze) indicates whether or not all three partners are able to create a shared focus of attention.
4. Facial expression + voice = *affective contact*: expressive behavior indicates (similar to dyadic play) whether or not each partner is able to initiate, develop and maintain affective contact and thus emotional intimacy.

When playing in the triad, the respective partners must therefore attune themselves to different physical levels. The critical *involvement* of all participants for a shared joyful game first of all depends on the physical orientation of pelvis and legs to each other. *Without the physical attunement from orientation by turning towards the other person with the lower body and without the affection by leaning forward with the upper body at a reasonable distance, no common focus of attention can be created by the coordination of gaze directions, and no mimical affect attunement can arise as well.* Metaphorically speaking, affect attunement, like the tip of the iceberg, cannot appear above the surface of perception if the interaction between the physical attunements – like the main part of the iceberg – did not exist below the water's surface.

It should be mentioned that the research of Beebe and Lachmann on interactive regulation in the dyad work just as early in the 2nd –3rd ML and with the same paradigm of joy in shared play as the "primary triangle" research. In the meantime, Beebe and colleagues (2010, 2014) also report that not only the rhythms of gaze sequences but the patterns of *contact and touch* (and thus *skin contact*) as well within a mother-child dyad at 4 months of age can also help to predict either a secure or a disorganized attachment at the age of one year. The dynamic developmental trajectory of bodily collaboration or co-operation in the further course of development in infants has been researched by Downing (2006, 2007). He refers to the process of the rhythms of physical dialogue in connection with the rhythms of affective exchange as "micro-practices." How both developmental trajectories unfold their effect and significance together is depicted in the studies conducted by Tomasello (2009). He describes mimical *and* gestural-physical attunements as the basis for the development of symbol formation and language. Accordingly, it is in the "primary triangle" that we first begin to anchor ourselves in our first social community/group, namely within the family. This is the beginning of growing into our culture, our language and into our higher cognitive functions. Tomasello (2009) speaks of the formation of a common (social) experiential background – a "common ground."

2.3. Primary Triangle and the Oedipus Myth

The research on the primary familial triangle has shown us that the entire family and their cooperation are important. *Affect attunement thereby proves to be rooted in physical attunement.* As early as during or even before pregnancy, the preconceptions of parents about their future joint care for their infant can be used to predict their later real cooperation and hence how the developmental fate of their yet unborn child will look like (cf. Klitzing, 2002). This is reminiscent of the Oracle of Delphi who predicted the fate of the not yet conceived Oedipus to his parents. According to this view, it is not the ancient gods (or drives) who determine[2] the tragic fate of a person in advance. It is rather the type of relationships, the affection, cooperation and empathy of the parents for their infant that determine a person's developmental fate.

When we take a look at the Oedipus myth (Schwab, 2008) in this light, then the instinct-driven internal conflicts and repressions in the soul of a man are not the most important aspects here in my opinion. Rather, the myth describes the tragic pre-oedipal, early childhood developmental fate of Oedipus as a result of the lack of love and cooperation between his parents. According to the *bodily organizational principles* as we find them described in the primary triangle, the early trauma of Oedipus in the myth is represented by his pierced feet (Clauer, 2011). This is pure symbolism without any comprehensible real need. To kill a young infant, it is enough to abandon it, as in the Oedipus saga, to a wild mountain landscape. From a bioenergetic-analytical point of view, however, I see this as a symbol of how the early trauma prevents the adult Oedipus from being well anchored or grounded in his own bodily self-experience, in his emotions and in his relationships, thus as his inability to stand on the ground of reality, which is characterized by social relationships. This social ground of reality Oedipus had problems to recognize clearly in the myth and we might say that his social intelligence had not developed well. This is symbolized by the fact that he put himself to blindness. The trauma and impairment to his development from the lack of loving cooperation and coordination between his parents in the myth eventually leads to the hateful-impetuous nature of Oedipus – this does not result in a mental malformation of instinct-driven fates.

2.4. Empathy, Affect Attunement and Physical Coordination in Psychotherapy

Besides introspection, it is empathy that has been emphasized by self-psychology as a central factor of psychotherapy. Self-psychology most often assumes that observing a face and facial expressions will reveal the inner life of a person (cf.

2 The topic of a predetermined fate or of aspirations and actions as a point of view has become topical again from the discussion of a neurobiologically influenced determinism.

Milch, 2001), as also suggested by the work of Krause (1983) and Darwin (1872). However, the trialogue game reveals that without the physical attunement from an orientation by turning towards the other person with the lower body and affection by leaning forward with the upper body at a reasonable distance, a common focus of attention cannot be achieved by coordinating gaze directions and facial attunement. This does not become immediately apparent in dyadic infant research and is taken for granted. This creates the false impression that the entire attunement and development process solely occurs by mimical affect attunement alone. Recent research, in contrast, shows that we can meaningfully decipher facial signals only in the overall context of the significance of physical signals (Aviezer et al., 2012; Herrmann, 2012). This is comparable to the fact that all the sensory signals from our large sensory organs, like our eyes and ears, only receive meaning within the context of proprioception together with tactile and vestibular sensations (i. e. the body's inner signals) and especially within the context of physical motion signals (Clauer, 2009a). This also means that the physical movements and signals of the entire body are more important for the attunement processes in our relationships than is often assumed (cf. Clauer, 2013b).

The interactions and attunement sequences between mother and infant are first of all a process on the implicit-procedural level. Feelings and posture patterns can also be conveyed in the psychotherapeutic treatment situation via the physical resonance processes of empathy, the embodied countertransference. I understand empathy in terms of sensitivity towards and feeling into the other person as a process of physical co-vibration or a coming into resonance with the non-conscious reality and the feelings of another person (Clauer, 2003; Heinrich, 1997; Heinrich-Clauer, 2008, Lewis, 2005). Psychoanalytic authors often emphasize the cognitive components of empathy (e.g. Barwinski, 2014). Empathy is described as a complex process that not only involves *affect resonance* but also a perspective assumption as *prosocial* behavior and *cognitive processes* of comprehending interpreting (Milch, 2001; Kilian & Köhler, 2013). As a Bioenergetic analyst, I emphasize corporal-emotional resonance as the implicit-procedural root of empathy. For about 15 years, I have explored the processes of an empathy understood as embodied resonance and of embodied countertransference (cf e.g. Clauer & Heinrich, 1999; Clauer, 2003, 2008, 2009a, 2013b, c).

According to Schore (2005, 2011), the cerebral processing of these embodied exchange processes is lateralized in the right brain and is predominant in the first one and a half to two years of an infant's life. Similarly, the right hemisphere is also ascribed a functional dominance in regulating the autonomous (organ) functions and the primary emotions (Porges, 2010, p. 76). The transmission of implicit knowledge and relationship knowledge from one person to another was also referred to by Schore (2005, 2011) as communication from the right side to the right side of the brain.

Mindfulness training for the implicit bodily processes – such as Bioenergetic analyst training – therefore makes it easier for therapists to understand how the patient is doing, how he is feeling. An empathic attitude is determined by a constant attentiveness to the *embodied relationship statements*. The facial expressions, gestures, posture, eye expressions, voice and breathing rhythms of the therapist and patient influence one another (cf. Zaccagnini, 2008). Less intersubjectively described but similarly, Koehler says that feelings which cannot be verbally transmitted are introduced into therapeutic situations by acting out, by facial expressions, movements, motoric restlessness and physical reactions such as sweating, palpitations and dizziness (cf. Milch, 2001, p. 283). The work of Rizzolatti (1999) and others have validated the respective motoric, sensory and affective processes (Bastiaansen et al., 2009) with mirror neurons and a process of embodied simulation, the model of the "embodied simulation" (Gallese, 2009). In the end, this means that a psychobiologically attuned therapist can become the interactive regulator of the experiential world of his patient (cf. Tonella, 2008, p. 64).

Beebe and Lachmann (2002, p. 35, 143f.) described key points that are of crucial importance to both dyadic and triadic attunement processes and for adult psychotherapy[3] as well:

- Ongoing intertwined nonverbal (and verbal) patterns of self-regulation and interactive regulation.
- Interruption and restoration of ongoing regulations.
- Increased affective moments.

These principles apply to both verbal and non-verbal regulatory paths. Regulation is organized according to these principles and the internalization of these kinds of patterns of experience is co-created.

The processes and organizational principles of embodied resonance are the basis for the exchange and interactive regulation between parents and infant not only. They are for sure the basis for access to early, implicit unconscious personality traits

3 I have also addressed the significance of these attunement principles in my psychoanalytic dissertation: Clauer, J. (2007): Anyone who shows emotions has lost. On the co-construction of healing rhythms in analytical psychotherapy of a patient with structural problems.

and disorders in the cohesion of self-experience to arise within the therapist-patient interaction too.

Embodied resonance can ultimately be consciously understood in the mutual therapy process. This most often is an integrative achievement by the therapist to understand these processes in a decryptive manner (to decipher them) and, if necessary, to reflect them verbally – *the empathic insight can but must not be symbolized and verbally formulated* (cf. Lyons-Ruth, 1999)! This kind of understanding shifts the focus and importance from the psycho-dynamic contents to the interactive (bodily) *forms and types of communicative exchange* within psychotherapies. The interactive forms of communicative exchange will be a focus of my observations in the case studies.

3. The Neurobiological Perspective

3.1. Self-Perception and Consciousness

To neurobiologist Damasio (2000, 2011) and to Metzinger (2005, 2009), self-perception/emerging sense of self, primal emotions, consciousness and spirit do not primarily arise as a function of the cerebral cortex: "Although the cerebral cortex is an important part of this system, I believe the brainstem to be the foundation of the self-process" (Damasio, 2011, p. 206). The received afferent information from the body, particularly the interoceptive information that is transmitted via the vagus from the internal organs, lead – based on the brain stem – to a proto sense of self that is associated with background feelings/vitality affects. The proto self emerges as a product of the integration of multiple sensory body perceptions, especially from the inner milieu of the bodily fluids and organs, the tactile sense of the skin, kinesthetic signals of the musculoskeletal system and the vestibular organ. This integration is in many ways "susceptible to interference," especially in the brainstem (ibid., p. 265). "The self is incrementally constructed on the foundation of the proto self" (ibid., p. 34). *The information of our body system as a whole is therefore closely linked to our vitality affects and is the basis of the development of consciousness and a sense of self.* In turn, the described vitality affects remind us of the important vitality contours in infant development by Stern (1986, 2011).

Only the change of the proto-self by interaction with objects can give rise to the pulses of a core self-perception that is capable of consciousness. *Self-perception and consciousness are therefore tied to an interaction*, the exchange with objects or persons. This model thus confirms self-psychological/intersubjective perspectives in which the patient and therapist unavoidably influence each other and co-create their conscious experience. Fragmentations and other self-experience disturbances are thus distinguished by the fact that the joint interactions and attunement processes are disturbed and must be restored. In the case of psychosomatic fragmentations it seems to me that a retreat into a forced self-regulation caused by developmental trauma takes place for the sake of ensuring the survival. However, an existential achievement of mammals no longer comes into play: the chances of survival and the welfare of mammals improve considerably from life and attunement in the group.

Self-perception and affects are thus inextricably tied to interactions, and without movement, no meaningful information can arise from our sensorial perceptions of the world. Only the internal or external movement of a vital, vibrant body leads to the perception and consciousness of a coherent self in its relatedness to the environment. A withdrawal from environmental stimuli soon leads to a fragmentation of self-experience. The rootedness in our bodily self-perception thus determines how we find our way in the world, how we navigate it (Damasio, 2000, 2011). The movements and impressions of our body form the basis for our sense of self. *When this physical anchor is lost, we also lose the coherence/integration of the self (-experience)*. Winnicott (1974, p. 193f.) already provides similar approaches:

> "The true self comes from the vitality of the body tissues and the activities of bodily functions, including the heart's activity and breathing. […] The true self appears as soon as there is any mental organization of the individual whatsoever, and it means little more than the totality of sensomotoric vitality."

It should be noted that self-perception and conscious self-awareness is inextricably tied to basic experience of affects. In treating psychosomatic patients it is also important to know that the emerging self-perception/sense of self and affective experience is intertwined with the vegetative regulation via the vagus complex i. e. the autonomic nervous system (ANS), at the brain stem level. Moreover, the vagus complex, i. e. the vagus and other cranial nerves[4], are also involved in regulating the mimic facial muscles and the muscles for swallowing, phonation and hearing.

4 The vagus and other cranial nerves (such as the trigeminal, facial, glossopharyngeal nerves) are tied with evolutionary developments from the branchial arch.

In this way, the emerging self-experience (and consciousness) is coupled with basal affects and the facial expression on the brainstem level, and it is closely tied to the vital-vegetative regulation of the functions of our internal organs and with social interaction. Figure 2 attempts to depict relevant nuclei in the brainstem for that, but not connections to other brain areas relevant for a more complex sense of self.

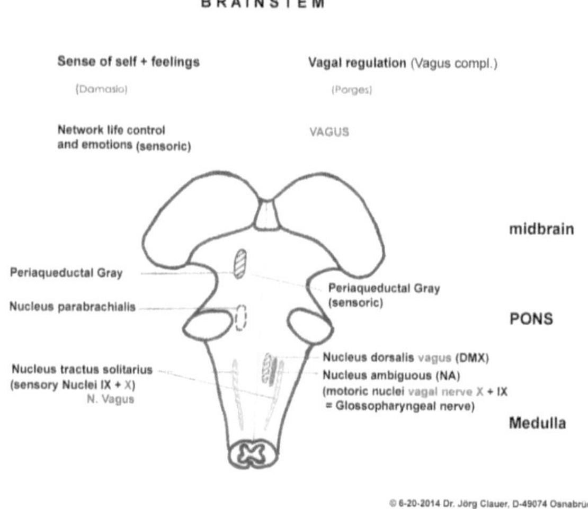

Figure 2. Brainstem © 6/20/2014. (according to Ferner & Staubesand, 1973; Porges, 2010; Damasio, 2011)

3.2. Prosocial Ventral Vagus Complex(VVC).

Porges' (2010) Polyvagal Theory differentiated the vagus in such a way that we can no longer assume the duality of a sympathetic and parasympathetic nervous system today, but rather a *tripartite autonomic nervous system* (ANS) as depicted in figure 3. In doing so, Porges employs the concept of neuroception and thus refers to an unconscious, continuously-vigilant scanning of the safety situation in our social environment.

Figure 3. Tripartite autonomic nervous system (ANS) © 9/23/2011. (according to Porges, 2010; Reich, 1972), presented at the 21st International Conference for Bioenergetic Analysis in San Diego/California

A psycho-vegetative situation to a moderate level of arousal and a trusting sense of safety is controlled by the ventral vagal complex (VVC) in the brainstem. This *ventral vagal complex* (VVC) is comprised of a myelinated vagus part from a ventral original core, the nucleus ambigus (NA), and cores of the trigeminus and facial nerves. The VVC is clearly related to the expression and experience of emotions (ibid., p. 77). When operating in its environmental perception of safety mode, it employs its so-called *VAGAL BRAKE* to *inhibit* an *increased level of arousal and the mobilizing flight and fight readiness of the sympathetic nervous system* (ibid., e.g. p. 249). Under the influence of the vagal brake, the *dorsal vagal core* (DVC) in turn stimulates the regenerative digestive processes during safe, resting situations. But when it is intensely stimulated under existentially threatening situations as the ventral vagal brake is released, the dorsal vagal core (DVC) then controls immobilizing, constrictive or dissociative reactions during life-threatening situations. Besides shock-induced paralysis, it can then engender pathological phenomena such as stomach ulcers, intestinal inflammation or sleep disorders. The ability of social engagement ("System Social Engagement," ibid.,

p. 174f.) that is connected to VVC-function depends on how we influence our facial and cranial muscles with the aid of neural pathways that connect the cortex and the brainstem (the cortico-bulbar pathways). These muscles make our face expressive and allow us to communicate meanings by gestures, to influence the sound of our voice, to turn our gaze to certain things and to distinguish human voices from background noise with our hearing. If the ventral vagus complex is constricted during a situation that is experienced as potentially life-threatening, then the neural regulation of the mimical facial muscles and cranial muscles, and thus perception and affective expression, are impaired as is often the case in psychosomatic illnesses such as alexithymia. Alexithymia refers to the inability to perceive or to read feelings. Bioenergetic analysts see a link here to the concept of "cephalic shock" as introduced by Robert Lewis (2008).

3.3. Psychotherapeutic Consequences

In summary, empathy with the bodily experiences and emotions of the infant (or the patient) establishes the ground or secure basis for the development of his/her self-awareness and self-esteem. To establish a sense of safety for the infant through interactive regulation also always means to regulate fear, anger and over-excitation. This follows a pattern: the child leads – the mother follows (cf. Schore, 2005).

If the environment is not attuned, hostile or insufficiently sensitive and non-empathetic in terms of cooperation during infancy, then impairments or trauma may result. Corresponding repetitive violations of empathy *from withdrawal by the caregiver and abandonment* or by not corrected/restored misattunements lead to hyper- or hypoarousal and, in time, to mental and anatomically tangible changes. The absent sense of safety in the relationship, which corresponds to a lack of secure attachment or experience of a reliable self-object, leads to a loss of trust in interactive regulation, and can lead to a retreat into a forced self-regulation and/or the urge and attempt to control the hostile experienced environment/reference persons as comprehensively as possible. This can easily go along with hyperarousal and fight or flight reactions, as we will see in my first case description. If the attempt at interactive control fails, then fragmentation reactions, a sense of powerlessness and devitalization can arise, as in the second case description.

Even if disturbed patients with early developmental traumas frequently have a pronounced desire for human empathy, understanding and backing or support, they exhibit a lack of confidence and security in the human group. Porges describes something similar in his model of neuroception and emphasizes that early disturbed patients with developmental trauma in particular easily misinterpret the attentiveness and attention of a psychotherapist on the subconscious level. Even the friendly facial expressions, voice or benevolent attitude of the therapist often seems not to reassure. His proximity is experienced as a threat or even as an existential threat. With this core idea, Porges (2010), in line with trauma therapists like van der Kolk, concludes that dialogical and especially verbal psychotherapy not only do not reach these kinds of patients, but even harms them and could retraumatize them. Porges thus recommends music therapy as the method of choice.

Thus he points to the fact that resonance and attunement to rhythmic bodily experiences like music can be helpful for those patients in particular. In addition to a support in this way, my experience is that disorders incurred in relationships need to be cured in relationships finally. Yet, as therapists of these kinds of patients we find ourselves in a situation that I compare with the image of an iceberg.[5] On the explicit level of conscious awareness and in the verbal dialogue of the talking cure, we are predominantly aware of the small proportion of the patient's self that is visible above the water. With our bioenergetic-analytical radar systems, we try to infer the large proportion under water, the implicit, embodied experience area, the implicit relational knowledge (cf. Clauer, 2013b). However, in the icy regions of people with a severely wounded self-experience we always run the risk of running aground with our own implicit-procedural, unconscious portion under water and of sinking on a traumatized patient iceberg that was shock-frozen in its early experience. That means to fail as a self-object and not being able to restore relatedness and attunement after inevitable breaches of the interaction.

For this to happen less frequently, all dialogical psychotherapies like bioenergetic analysis and self-psychology, according to my experience, provide a great opportunity to not only incorporate empathy and empathic affect attunement but psychotherapeutic collaboration/cooperation as well and thus the entire (potential) space of implicit-procedural processes within the therapeutic relationship. The collaborative attunement processes are not only the basis of body psychotherapeutic ways of working. Its importance was also emphasized by Lyons-Ruth (1999, cited from Lachmann, 2010 p. 93f.) that

> "systems of meaning are organized to capture implicit or procedural forms of knowledge. Enactive processes can be better articulated and integrated by participating in more coherent and collaborative forms of intersubjective interaction. In order

5 The image of the iceberg is familiar to me from a paper by Shapiro (2000).

> to promote therapeutic care, these enactive processes do not necessarily need to be translated into reflexive symbolic knowledge or verbalized. The *collaborative process,* which incorporates the dialogue between patient and analyst as much as enactments do, helps to foster its 'implicit relational knowledge.'"

I want to demonstrate how this may look like based on the following two case descriptions. In the first case of a patient with a predominantly psychosomatic fragmentation, the main focus is on the security of self-experience and existence by controlling the therapeutic situation or scene. In the second case of a patient with a complex fragmentation, the main focus is on collaboration and rhythmic bodily attunement processes. Both patients have suffered a variety of traumas in their life histories.

4. Case Histories

4.1. 1st Case: A Psychosomatic Case History – from the Self-Regulating Organ Mode to the Interactive Mode

When the patient came to me at about 39 years of age, his ulcerative colitis had flared up massively after conflicts with his male boss. He took cortisone and azathioprine, an immunosuppressant used for intestinal inflammation. A behavioral therapy had proven ineffective.

The parents were very young when he was born and quarrelsome. They did not cooperate and had no loving relationship. They were only sporadically present. Often he was at his discontented grandmother together with his younger sister. According to this background, to protect him from his violent father, he was sent by his mother and grandmother between the age 10 and 17 to a Catholic boarding school where he was sexually abused by a priest. Exhibiting an open bisexual orientation, he is married and has two daughters.

4.1.1. On the Course of Therapy: A Painstaking Birth – Reviving Mutual Regulation

Phase 1: Adapting Yourself to the Patient

As a sign of his alexithymia, the patient could not communicate anything about his anxiety and other emotions. Instead, he repeatedly spoke of an inner emptiness. At the end of the therapy he said: "The most difficult part for me was to perceive my actual affectivity and emotional equilibrium. Until now, I had to control my environment with great vigilance and keep a look out for any escape routes. This minimized the danger that my fears would attack my gut in milliseconds." His constant readiness to fight was intended to prevent him from experiencing himself completely at the mercy in relationships, of losing control and self-regulation and that it "went right into his pants," as he said and this caused him tremendous shame. To achieve a sense of safety whenever he found himself in new surroundings, he had to first find out where the nearest toilet was.

Right away he had a strong urge to control the time frame and spatial organization of our setting. Particularly in the initial phase of the therapy did he insist on frequent, even longer "work-related" interruptions of our therapy sessions. I was only able to achieve certain continuity in the therapy sessions by reacting very flexibly to his scheduling demands. He himself quickly remembered the story of Oedipus and threatened me indirectly with something similar to the fate of that father: in case of any dispute over the arrangement of the relationship, he would cut me out of his life by discontinuing the therapy. I often found it hard to overcome my anger about being coerced in such a way and every now and then called into question the controlling nature of the relationship arrangement. Sometimes I needed my supervisor in order not to try to employ "gentle force" on my part to urge the patient to do something like an extension of the therapy which he considered to be long superfluous. Only after a period of almost three years did he also succeeded in recalling positive experiences with his father and said: "Instead of hate mongering, I frequently have compassion for my father now."

To avoid being other-directed again, the patient frequently exhibited no attunement with me as regards the change of speaker. I then had the feeling, with my impulses to say something, of standing opposite a tightly woven curtain of his uninterrupted flow of words that seemed to spill out at me like the wall of a waterfall. I felt other-directed again in the course of this scenario and had the impression that my feeling was probably something similar to what the patient had felt in his own childhood.

We initially sat diagonally opposite each other. Later on, after some experiments with the setting, he selected a spot at a right angle, laterally removed on the therapy mat. He often looked straight ahead in that position and not at me. Here, too, I registered a "rumbling" in my belly after some period of time. I addressed this in a playful manner at some point, and also started to look straight ahead. In doing so, I cast doubt on the one sided interactive regulation. He was extremely irritated by this and protested vehemently. He wanted my continuous undivided attention (with the option that only he could look away). However, the question regarding how he had experienced the situation and me and the enquiry into our interaction led to a restoration of the attunement and made the reciprocity of the attunement more conscious.

Besides the aforementioned averted gaze, *running away* was also an important relationship regulation for him. Whenever he became overexcited, he would abruptly run to the bathroom. I felt some empathy for his somatic-vegetative need and the threat of shame in remembering a time of dysentery in my life. My benevolently communicated acceptance of this "regulation" was important to him in order that he experienced himself as understood and accepted, as he related to me. Beside that it was hard work for me to accept him rejecting all exercises and physical contact offered by me. Even during colitis flare ups he refused any soothing physical contact (a kind of contact I used in a former case of ulcerative colitis; Clauer, 2008). This provoked feelings of being helpless and impotent as a Bioenergetic Analyst. He also continuously rejected all other physical interactions and also avoided any expression of emotion. But through the body psychotherapeutic endeavors, he clearly realized that any notion of physical proximity to me was tied to a fear of losing control, of helplessness and the expectation of a great threat.

Phase 2: Proximity and Emotional Neglect

A major turning point came after almost two years and from an entirely surprising incidence to both of us. Just before my vacation, I went to see a doctor and unexpectedly met the patient there early in the morning. We were alone in the waiting room. I was puzzled and felt insecure how to react with a kind of tightness. For sure I greeted him and then sat down at some distance, but inevitably at a right angle to him, like in our therapeutic setting. It was an uncomfortable ambivalent situation. The unexpected proximity led to an acute episode of his ulcerative colitis.

After my vacation, he told about the first outbreak of his illness for the first time. He succeeded to be expelled from boarding school by stealing and then lived at his grandmother's. Yet his attempt to graduate from high school failed. After his subsequent civilian service, he stayed in the Holstein area, apprenticed there as a plumber and lived with his first girlfriend. He remembered that he had felt completely uprooted after finally moving out of his parents', who he vehemently rejected. The parents of the girlfriend, in contrast, showed kind feelings to him. It was during this time in his apprenticeship and with his girlfriend that the disease now broke out. The desire at that time for a secure relationship regulation and a secure bond were hardly reconcilable with the fear of a loss of autonomy and self-regulation.

After the encounter in the doctor's waiting room, he also arrived to the next session after my vacation with a dream that best captured his affliction. In the dream, he discovered a corpse embedded in concrete in the floor of a hidden basement room. The description was so vivid as if we were both standing together in this basement room. For the first time, he also described a feeling, namely: "*to be emotionally encased in concrete.*"

Phase 3: Coordinated Activities and the Thawing of Emotional Worlds

In my next vacation a few weeks later I had hiked over the Alps. Directly upon our first greeting, he inquired about my vacation experience. Contrary to my analytical habit and surprise, I gave him a spontaneous, direct, authentic response. After this response, he developed the image of us on a joint Alpine hike and of using me as a scout on his path.

During the course of our hike, we encountered – like in his dream – a frozen corpse in the ice, an "Ötzi," or iceman. He now experienced the process of a slow physical and emotional thawing connected to the emerging memories of his experiences of abuse. We understood our surprising proximity in the doctor's waiting room as the trigger for his remembered experiences of abuse. In the further course of his treatment, he took advantage of opportunities to also process the abuse via the court system.

I can also remember situations on our joint hike where tears, which the patient could not yet cry, came to my eyes when I experienced empathy with him emotionally abandoned and lonely in the Catholic boarding school for instance. He seemed to notice this and later reported that he was now able to weep at home with his wife following any moving or emotional therapy process. At the end of the therapy we then experienced that he could cry tears in my presence.

Phase 4: Opening the Door for Mutual Regulation

The common experiences in the therapy process and during the imaginary hike had led to a secure experience basis. Our attention now turned to a social third party – the escalating conflict with his boss. He experienced her to be as possessive as his mother was, felt emotionally abused, and fought a long, tough and fierce battle with her. Contrary to my fears, the changes achieved so far remained stable.

After quitting and receiving his severance pay, this dispute finally ends one year later. What remained was an issue which he described using a picture from a book: a *"porte recondamnée,"* i.e. a safety door like the kind used in the food industry, which can only be opened from the inside with a horizontal handlebar. *His solitary anguished self-regulation as a safeguard against his feeling of being threatened by his surroundings had now received a handy (and great) symbolization in the truest sense of the word.* In this last phase of the therapy he could finally allow to be emotionally touched as well, allow tears and bodily contact and feel compassion for his father. He tried his best to meet my available appointment dates. In his desire for a sense of solidarity, he was able to open the symbolic, one-sided inner door and allow moments of powerlessness and helplessness.

I was particularly pleased by the fact that his gastroenterologist had diagnosed a healthy intestine during a colonoscopy 6 months prior to the end of his therapy. This finding also persisted without the need for any additional medication. Our farewell after the long hike was moving for both of us.

4.1.2. Commentary on the Therapy Process

According to Sander as well as Beebe and Lachmann, *temporal, spatial and affective attunements* and joint (movement) rhythms are effective organizational principles of communication *throughout life*. When we transfer Sander's descriptions of problems in the development of the mother-infant dyad onto the therapist-patient dyad, some similarities can be found for the aforementioned therapy process.

The first phase of therapy, however, can be understood as a covert struggle over access to an interactive regulation. The patient exhibited at different levels a great effort to control the time frame and the spatial organization of our settings. My first response or countertransference to this scenario, with the angry feelings, corresponded to his implicit and then also verbally stated experience and threat of an oedipal struggle for power and dominance with me as the therapist-father. I also found this very pronounced in his one-sided and often lacking temporal attunement regarding the change of speaker. It is known that this kind of lack of attunement triggers very aversive feelings that I myself could not escape from. Had I primarily let myself into this fight mode and not contained or processed/digested this ire, then the patient would have terminated the relationship/therapy as he threatened to do.

The initial phase can also be understood and regarded in a different way. He had described that his parents were young, overwhelmed and at odds with each other. So there was not much loving cooperation between them or much affection for him. As in my alternative assessment of the Oedipus myth (cf. 2.3.), it is obvious that the patient was disturbed/traumatized early on in his self-development. The organ mode of his colitis can thus be seen as a (controlled by the dorsal vagus) shameful emergency response to a threat. The patient tried to prevent its occurrence by a forced control of his environment. The nature of this *"vegetative relationship regulation"* can be compared to Sander's 1st phase of the primary regulation of biological processes for maintaining homeostasis. Like the mother who must attune herself to her baby in the first phase of life, I felt prompted by him at the beginning of our work process to largely adjust my practice organization to his temporal, spatial, physical and affective rhythms (according to the "child leads, mother follows" formula). If a mother does not adjust herself to the needs of her infant so that it then experiences itself as neglected, other-directed, overwhelmed or threatened, then the baby is only left with an inner withdrawal from the relationship with his unsuccessful protest. Similarly, the patient repeatedly expressed that the therapeutic relationship would be interrupted or aborted should I not adapt myself to his "needs." Like mothers experience it from time to time, I sometimes developed a distinct reluctance or annoyance at the efforts involved in making these adjustments. The importance of implicit nonverbal cooperative path of relational attunement processes in the psychotherapy of "difficult patients" on the levels of temporal patterns, spatial relatedness, affective arousal and physically-proprioceptive stimulation have also been pointed out by Kiersky and Beebe (1994, p. 390). A similar position can be found in Massimo Ammaniti (2009), who points to the importance of physical attunement processes in psychotherapeutic processes.

My mostly *adequate adjustment* to his needs had paved the way for changes and developments in the relationship. His influence on our relationship formation gradually fostered a sense of safety in the relationship and a feeling of participation as well as authorship and agency – in place of the fear of his overwhelming helplessness and powerlessness. I regard his initiative to select another spot as a sign of increasing security. This selection had given him new ways of regulating eye contact and attention in our working relationship. It was now easier for him to either isolate himself or to turn towards me. This ensured his participation in the relationship regulation. It was in his hands to direct his attention/turn towards me and he was able to further unfold a *feeling of self-efficacy(agency)/authorship* instead of powerlessness *with the no of his averted gaze.*

All in all, this therapy phase again and again showed indications and elements of Sander's descriptions of phases 2 + 3 regarding the development of reciprocal exchange and the initiative of the child (cf. Sander, 2009 p. 318f.). In particular, the reciprocal rhythmic relatedness with gaze aversion is identified by Sander as part of the reciprocal exchange of physical activities. My averted gaze put into question the rather one-sided interactive regulation in which he led and I followed. When we examined his protest of my averted gaze, this returned my attention back to him and gave me a little more room to play in as a step towards greater perceived reciprocal regulation. The negotiation over boundaries and influence in the relationship continued to foster a sense of security, self-confidence and, above all, his own self-efficacy/authorship. My interventions like my gaze aversion can be compared to "Ferenczi's active technique" (2004). They enabled an unfolding of interactive regulation processes in the therapeutic dyad during the further course of the treatment which were reminiscent of Sander's problems 5–7 (cf. chapter 2.1.).

A respective phase-specific potential embodied *"NO"* is of great importance to the development of agency and autonomy. Fig. 1 tries to show phase specific differences of a *"NO"* in that way. In the beginning, he had threatened me with the complete break-up of the relationship – similar to how an infant may initially do so with a complete inward retreat in the form of "glassy eyes" whenever his cries (also known as a cry baby) show no practical success (cf. Stern, 1986). In addition to the exhibited *"NO by gaze aversion,"* he still exhibited the *"motoric NO by running away"* to the bathroom. These interactions can be seen as stages of a development towards autonomy. Only much later, during the period of his struggle with his female boss, was the *"verbal mode of NO"* at the focus of his development.

At the beginning of our mutual process, the patient quickly felt himself at the mercy of the situation. His subsequent description of the constant watchful control of his environment in this phase of the therapy is reminiscent of Porges' (2010) description of neuroception. My experience of the relationship and his subsequent descriptions suggest that he found himself in a constant fight and flight readiness when scanning his surroundings and thereby neurovegetatively in a state of SNS hyperarousal. Any movement that came too close to him and questioned his control of the social environment (i. e. with his boss as he often reported and the therapist as well) immediately triggered a reaction that matched a regulation by the dorsal vagus (DVC). He quickly experienced himself existentially threatened and his gut took control of regulating (proximity and) distance in a relationship with these diarrheal attacks. I myself experienced an ambivalence to stay at a distance he was able to tolerate and an impulse to offer to him a soothing bodily dialogue or "empathic contact" especially in times of his colitis flare ups (as I knew it to be effective from a former case of ulcerative colitis, Clauer, 2008). This relational problem Porges maybe addresses in his neurobiological understanding. His proposal to intervene with music therapy might have been another way to soothe the relational tension I felt and towards a solution of the intersubjective problems.

In our case we took another way. The unconsciously initiated and controlled early developmental processes described by the patient were then followed by the surprising situation in the doctor's waiting room with his resulting reaction in the organ mode, a colitis flare-up. His unexpected inquiry about my vacation experiences allowed him, unlike in the doctor's waiting room, to re-establish the initiative and control. When I opened myself up to his question and spontaneously gave him an authentic response and thus relinquished my boundaries and control, could he then risk the joint Alpine hike. He could now use me as a scout, as he said, as a useful self-object. In his conception of the mountain hike, it was a first confirmation that we were on our way to establish a physical cooperation and mutual affect regulation. This is reminiscent of Sander's 3rd and 4th initiative phases (which already occurred when he selected the seated position) and the focus on my availability and limitations as relationship partner during our long, imagined mountain hike. Even emergent memories of abuse and the thawing of his emotional shock-induced paralysis were now possible, which – also viewed with the neuroception model – appears as a confirmation of the increasing social security within our relationship. Witnessing my expressions of emotion like my tears, probably also helped the patient out of his emotional freeze. Naming feelings was certainly not decisive in this alexithymia patient. He benefited much more from witnessing my expressions of emotion which reflected his incommunicable or not perceived emotions. The shared experiences during the (imaginary) hike also created, considering Tomasello's (2009) work, the shared basis for a common language of emotion and compassion, and thus a change in his alexithymia.

In the last therapy phase while struggling with his female boss, the issues of Sander's phases 5–7 emerged even more than in our direct interaction. It was a tough struggle for his self-assertion in opposition to the boss (phase 5). In doing so, he took advantage of the resulting security in his relationship to me in terms of a backing for an early triangulation. He also struggled for the (consciously experienced) attention of his intentions and the recognition of his delimited self. So it is understandable that he definitely experienced his termination of employment and separation as progress. He also regarded it as a step that confirmed his position and boundaries. It also concerned developmental issues which Sander refers to as recognition and continuity, as phase 6 and 7.

The patient thus felt sufficiently secure with me at the end of the hike during the time of the dispute with his boss – which was by the way a triangulated situation. This way it was possible that, despite the threatening and tense situations, his old patterns of SNS hyperarousal were no longer transferred into his customary shock frozen immobilization and the associated organ mode of the colitis regulated by the dorsal vagus (DVC), but could be regulated together socially and then increasingly abated.

4.2. 2nd Case: Bodily Cooperation and Psycho-Vegetative Regulation

4.2.1. Symptoms and Case History

This 44 year-old patient who was living alone came to psychotherapy with a severe recurrent depression with a morning low. Even as an adult, the woman who was often traumatized in childhood was accustomed to calming herself with jactitation, that is, with rocking motions. These self-reassurances were not enough to calm her down when her job situation aggravated. This came about by excessive demands, but especially by devaluating comments which threatened her unstable self-esteem again and again. Even hospital stays could not prevent further decompensations/autonomic dysfunctions. Since no more sleep function was eventually recorded at the sleep laboratory, she was forced into early retirement. An important resource to her were her singing skills, which she employed while playing in a women's cabaret up to her retirement.

She came with an evening medication of 125 mg of TAXILAN, 50mg of opipramol, promethazine (atosil) as needed and a 2 x 40 mg beta-blocker due to a hyperkinetic heart syndrome since the age of 18. A preceding bioenergetic psychotherapy and equine-facilitated therapy with my wife had enabled her to start psychotherapy with me as a male.

She grew up poor as the third of five children and the only girl. The parents suffered from alcohol dependency, attacked each other with knives and beat their children. The mother was particularly unfair. The children had to watch the father rape their mother. The only positive experience in her life was probably her living near grandmother. She had also won judo championships in her childhood which the father had encouraged until puberty. She said, "I functioned in life, finished school and my apprenticeship and have always worked. But I've very much still remained a child and never let myself in on sexuality. Since a longtime boyfriend betrayed me with my best girlfriend, I hold on tightly to my alcohol and cigarettes and withdraw myself from the world entirely."

4.2.2. The Course of Therapy: Coordinated Physical Cooperation

In the first few months she learned how to use the balance-disc, the Do-In (a structured self-massage that promotes the cohesion of self-experience and mindfulness: (cf. Clauer, 2009a, b; Kushi, 1994) and became familiar with and used for herself the safe internal place and vault for traumatized individuals. But none of these things led to any significant, lasting changes in her behavior or symptoms. Her inner experience only reorganized itself within our embodied relationship dialogue. We worked using rhythmic movements sitting back to back on a Pezziball (a gym-ball of a diameter of 50–80 cm), or I held her head and moved it gently back and forth while she lay on the therapy mat. As time went by she repeatedly requested this type of cooperation and nevertheless was so full of fear that her eyebrows vibrated and both our breath got caught mostly in the beginning when I held her head. As I grounded myself in my ischium-bones and relaxed my breathing she was able to relax slowly too more and more.

After many or, more specifically, more than one hundred "experiments" back to back or by holding and rhythmically moving her head, she became increasing relaxed in the therapy. Only now did she relate her periodic immersion in the parallel worlds of her girlhood dreams and about the true amount of her alcohol consumption.

4.2.3. Initiative and Self-Efficacy

She followed my intended movements on the Pezziball or relinquished her head to my hands for a long time. In doing so, she had adapted herself to my lead. Eventually she surprised me by saying that my predominant left-right movements on the ball were different from her own rocking – and she initiated back and forth movements. She talked about her sensations during the "experiments" and became more and more active. Out of her isolated, almost autistic seeming self-regulation via the jactitation came cooperative regulation and mutual attunement.

4.2.4. Dreams – Access to the Unconscious

She would now regularly bring her dreams to the session. An intense dream- analytical process developed that accompanied the body psychotherapeutic work, which later faded into the background. Her interest was now focused on our discussions about her dreams. She was pleasantly surprised by the, to her, new interest in the world of her inner experience and my response to it. She was increasingly fascinated by the joint journey into the often frightening world of her dreams in which she no longer felt alone now. In these dreams she was on the run[6] down the branching corridors, passageways and shafts of a menacing labyrinth, most of the time some vague subjects behind her. She was usually without orientation, found no way out and would finally wake up in cold sweat. This scenery and the process essentially stayed this way for a long period of time. But she now was able to share her hopeless experience with me and remembered similar feelings and the burdensome experience in her childhood and family.

It was a dense process of empathic sharing of experiences that she was until now completely isolated with, similar to her jactitation. Often I felt some tightness in my chest, my breath got caught again, it was too threatening and no way to scream and I had a sensation of being lost in space. Mostly I was busy to keep my breathing alive and to investigate and understand her dream situation in comparison with her life situation and her remembered childhood experience – and all in all to find with her some hope and confidence in change. I thereby overlooked almost a fundamental transformation that already took place: she was able to sleep again and therefore retain her dreams and bring these along with her. The physical fragmentations were thus abating. With further advances in the therapy, the dreams finally transformed: they became "brighter," with more and more orientation and finally with exits and ways out.

4.2.5. Vitality and Sexuality

In the further course of the therapy she could now also address her problems with sexuality. She stopped the alcohol abuse and reduced the medication to finally 50 mg TAXILAN besides the beta-blockers. Her sleep behavior was also improved under the reduced medication. She felt more agile and more alert during the day, mingled with people again, earned money for singing lessons and performed with a singing group. She found back to her own voice and rhythm after our reenacted rhythmic encounter. Finally, she met a partner with whom she "got to know sexuality as something enriching" for the first time in her life as she remarked. She has since married, resumed her work and is struggling to find solutions to the problems of her partner's sons.

Only at the end of the therapy did she finally told me that she had experienced

6 The impersonal pressure, excessive demands and lack of appreciation at her place of work in a spacious building were, besides being abandoned by her boyfriend and girlfriend, the main triggering factor for her decompensations.

herself in the figures of various famous men on a regular basis at the beginning of our collaboration – in terms of a multiple personality. These psychic fragmentations had disappeared according to her accounts at the beginning of her romantic relationship.

4.3. Comments on the 2nd Case History

The patient initially reported how she had learned to merely function in life and thus increasingly reported indirectly about her "false self." Her symptoms pointed to very basal "proximal" disturbances of vitality, self-awareness and self-regulation with effects on the vegetative level of the ANS with heart arrhythmia and sleep deprivation. This was tied to a great distrust of men and relationship, which corresponds to an impairment in the "Social Engagement System" in the neuroception model (see chapter 3.2.). The hyperkinetic heart syndrome is, according to Porges (2010), a clear indication of a chronic hyperarousal of SNS. Her traumatized psychobiological system was geared to a variety of potential risks. In light of a constantly experienced (or inwardly feared) threat, it is an adaptive response that the vagal brake and the mode of social trust were only very difficult to reactivate (cf. ibid., p. 251). The in her childhood multiply traumatized patient was accustomed to calming herself with jactitation, that is with rocking motions, even as an adult because she had not experienced calming experiences in relationships to a sufficient extent. The thus necessary self-reassurances from cradling or swinging movements are one of the most effective strategies of vagal stimulation and reactivation of the vagal brake (ibid., p. 233). But even these self-calming measures were insufficient when the situation escalated at her job. The excessive demands and especially the devaluations threatened the coherence of her fragile self and harmed it over and over again. Her existentially threatened self-experience was then left only to reactions controlled by the dorsal vagus (DVC) like hypoarausal with dissociations and a vegetative collapse with a lack of sleep, with panic and depression.

If we now follow Sander's (2009, cf. 2.1) developmental stages, then the self-experience and self-regulation of the patient as a truly "early disorder" were disturbed down into the first basal level of biological regulation. This was connected to the consequences as described by Schore (2005, 2011) and Porges (2010) of chronic hyperarousal (hyperkinetic heart syndrome) or eventually the symptoms of a controlled hypoarousal via the DVC. Since rocking motions are supposed to be very effective in stimulating the vagus, it is no wonder that the rhythmic attunement and action processes on the Pezziball or when holding and moving the head turned out to be particularly helpful. In a similar manner, parents soothe their infant with rocking movements in early infant development. According to Sander, these can be compared to the second phase of his classification and regarded as a reciprocally coordinated exchange of physical activities. They are also reminiscent of the protoconversations of Colwyn Trevarthen (2009) and the formation of repetitive patterns, i. e. of RIGs as described by Stern (1986). With the rhythmic movements, new repetitive patterns, new experiences of security and relaxation emerged within the therapeutic relationship in the course of our "one hundred experiments." This was a sufficiently secure basis for her impulses and communicated desires to find an affirmative response. It eventually led to a *qualitative envelope* where *initiative and self-efficacy* of the patient in the relationship to the therapist were able to develop and express themselves and received an inner self-confidence. This corresponds to Sander's phases three and four.

Likewise in Porges' (2010) preferred music therapy rhythmic processes exist that he says to be beneficial. In working with this patient, however, it were rhythmic bodily-cooperative attunements *within a dyadic therapeutic relationship* which had changed the regulation in the ANS in terms of a neuroception of safety and thus a reactivated vagal brake (Porges, 2010). As we see rhythmic processes in music therapy seem to be a valuable, helpful instrument in psychotherapy as well as rhythmic bodily processes within an embodied relational dialogue. The resulting sense of safety in the relationship can also reconcile or explain improved sleep and social activities with the neurobiological findings.

The process of rhythmic attunement and cooperation involved constant searching and was accompanied with feelings of great insecurity in me over a long period of time: afraid to either overwhelm her and conjur up catastrophic results or give in to a regressive maelstrom and sink into or get bogged down in it with the patient because – in addition to her desire for physical interaction – she regularly stressed that she would never work again. My analytic superego accused me of wish fulfillment and of complying with her regressive pursuit for amends. However, in time I understood her desire never to work again as a progressive, self-protecting attitude and differentiation from the devaluations at her job that had harmed her self-coherence and had triggered the decompensations. The patient herself had repeatedly very clearly expressed how beneficial our work was to her and that she only feared the curtailment of treatment by her health insurance. She had therefore been content with a frequency of only 2 hours a week.

The actively-induced action dialogues have therefore not, as often feared by psychoanalysts, constricted or even prevented the room for play, imagination and symbolization. On the contrary, the bodily experiences promoted new prosocial behavioral possibilities and opened up space for dream analysis and symbolization. Conflicts, for example regarding dependency versus autonomy, were thus made accessible to processing. Her new capacity for love thus proved to be a confirmatory expression and the result of this conversion and developmental process.

5. Conclusion

Employing the two dynamic trajectories of infant development can be of great value in psychotherapies of patients suffering from severe disorders or fragmentations of self. Those two are *affect attunement* that builds on the second one, the *physical cooperation and relational rhythms.* Self-awareness, affects and consciousness are tied to movement and interaction, the exchange with objects or persons. The rootedness in our bodily self-perception thus determines how we find our way in the world, how we navigate it. When this physical anchor is lost, we also lose the coherence/integration of the self (-experience). A withdrawal from environmental stimuli soon leads to a fragmentation of self-experience.

Comparable to the parent-infant interaction the temporal, spatial, affective and bodily proprioceptive *forms* of communicative modes of exchange and rhythms are of fundamental importance for the self-development of patients. They are the background for a process-oriented Bioenergetic analysis. The leading edge in this way is the embodied resonance (empathy) and bodily cooperation in the therapeutic dialogue which is considered as a mutual developmental process of the patient-therapist dyad. Similar to the situation of mother and baby we sometimes need to give into the patient leading the relational process. Like in the first case history all our exercises and bodily contact offered might be refused then. Nevertheless it is of great value to be in contact and resonate to patients with the full range of our embodied relational knowledge and an empathic attitude that is determined by a constant attentiveness to the embodied relationship statements. In the second case study we notice, according to the work of Porges, that regular rhythmic modes of bodily relational dialogues similar as music are of special value to change processes of patients with trauma and fragmentations.

This kind of comprehension shifts the focus *from psycho-dynamic contents* to the interactive (bodily) *forms and types of communicative exchange* within psychotherapies. The implicit nonverbal path of relational attunement and rhythms of cooperative bodily regulations are effective organizational principles of communication *throughout life* and in psychotherapy of "difficult patients" as well.

They are for sure the basis for access to early, implicit unconscious personality traits and disorders in the cohesion of self-experience to arise within the therapist-patient interaction too. To establish understanding for attunement and developmental processes within a therapeutic dialogue can promote the healing process in this perspective.

References

Ammaniti, M. (2009): Reply to Commentaries. Psychoanalytic Dialogues, 19, 585–587.

Ammaniti, M. & Trentini, C. (2009): How New Knowledge about Parenting Reveals the Neurobiological Implications of Intersubjectivity: A Conceptual Synthesis of Recent Research. Psychoanalytic Dialogues, 19, 537–555.

Aviezer, H.; Trope, Y. & Todorov, A. (2012): Body Cues, not Facial Expressions Discriminate between Intense Positive and Negative Emotions. Science, 338, 1225–1229.

Barwinski, R. (2014): Differenzierung der Gegenübertragung anhand entwicklungspsychologischer Konzepte. Psyche, 68, 517–536.

Bastiaansen, J. A. C. J.; Thioux, M.; Keysers, C. (2009) Evidence for mirror systems in emotions. Phil. Trans. R. Soc. B., 364, 2391–2404.

Beebe, B. & Lachmann, F. M. (2002): Infant Research and Adult Treatment: co-constructing interactions. Hillsdale, NJ, The Analytic Press. German: (2004): Säuglingsforschung und die Psychotherapie Erwachsener. Stuttgart: Klett-Cotta.

Beebe, B.; Jaffe, J.; Markese, S.; Buck, K.; Chen, H.; Cohen, P.; Bahrick, L.; Feldstein, S.; Andrews, H. (2010): The origins of 12-month attachment: A microanalysis of 4-month mother-infant interaction. Attachment and Human Development, 12, 1–135.

Beebe, B. & Lachmann, F. M. (2014): The Origins of Attachment: Infant Research and Adult Treatment. New York: Routledge.

Buti-Zaccagnini, G. (2008): Affektive Beziehungen und Körperprozesse. In: Heinrich-Clauer, V. (Hg): Handbuch Bioenergetische Analyse. Gießen, Psychosozial: 151–160. Engl. (2011): Affective Relationships and Bodily Processes. In: Heinrich-Clauer, V. (Ed): Handbook Bioenergetic Analysis. Gießen: Psychosozial-Verlag, 149–158.

Clauer, J. (2003): Von der projektiven Identifikation zur verkörperten Gegenübertragung: Eine Psychotherapie mit Leib und Seele. Psychother. Forum, 11, 92–100.

Clauer, J. (2008): Verkörpertes (leiblich-seelisches) Begreifen: Die Behandlung psychosomatischer Erkrankungen in der Bioenergetischen Analyse. In: Heinrich-Clauer, V. (Ed.): Handbuch Bioenergetische Analyse. Gießen, Psychosozial: 383–409. English: (2011): Embodied Comprehension: Treatment of Psychosomatic Disorders in Bioenergetic Analysis. In: Heinrich-Clauer, V. (Ed): Handbook Bioenergetic Analysis. Gießen: Psychosozial-Verlag, 369–394.

Clauer, J. (2009a): Zum Grounding-Konzept der Bioenergetischen Analyse: Neurobiologische und entwicklungspsychologische Grundlagen. Psychoanalyse & Körper 15(2): 79–102. English: (2011): Neurobiology and Psycholgical Development of Grounding and Embodiment. Bioenergetic Analysis, 21, 33–42.

Clauer, J. (2009b): Balancierscheibe und Baumübung. In: Fliegel, S. & Kämmerer, A. (Ed.): Psychotherapeutische Schätze II. Tübingen: dgvt-Verlag, 29–30.

Clauer, J. (2011): Kooperation in der Entwicklung des Menschen 1: Implikationen für die Bioenergetische Analyse. 2: Die Füße des Ödipus in neuen Schuhen. Forum Bioenergetische Analyse, 1, 42–89.

Clauer, J. (2013a): Psychovegetative Regulation, Kooperation, Triade und das Grounding-Konzept der Bioenergetischen Analyse. Thielen M (Ed.) Körper-Gruppe-Gesellschaft. Gießen: Psychosozial-Verlag, 277–286.

Clauer, J. (2013b): Die implizite Dimension in der Psychotherapie. In: Geißler, P.& Sassenfeld, A.(Hg): Jenseits von Sprache und Denken. Implizite Dimensionen im psychotherapeutischen Geschehen. Gießen: Psychosozial-Verlag, 135–173.

Clauer, J. (2013c): Das verkörperte Selbst: Empathie und Embodiment. körper – tanz – bewegung, 1, 13–20.

Clauer, J. & Heinrich, V. (1999) Körperpsychotherapeutische Ansätze in der Behandlung traumatisierter Patienten: Körper, Trauma und Seelenlandschaften. Zwischen Berührung und Abstinenz. Psychother Forum, 7, 75–93.

Damasio, A. R. (2000): Ich fühle, also bin ich. Berlin, List. Engl. (1999): The Feeling of what Happens. Body and Emotion in the Making of Consciousness. New York: Harcourt Brace & Company.

Damasio, A. R. (2011): Selbst ist der Mensch. München, Siedler. Engl. (2010): Self comes to Mind. Constructing the Conscious Brain. New York: Pantheon Books.

Darwin, C. (1872): The Expressions of the Emotions in Man and Animals. London, HarperCollinsPubl. German: (2000): Der Ausdruck der Gemütsbewegungen bei dem Menschen und den Tieren. Frankfurt/M.: Eichborn.

Downing, G. (2006): Frühkindlicher Affektaustausch und dessen Beziehung zum Körper. In: Marlock, G. & Weiss, H. (Eds.): Handbuch der Körperpsychotherapie. Stuttgart: Schattauer, 333–361.

Downing, G. (2007): Unbehagliche Anfänge: Wie man Psychotherapie mit schwierigen Patienten in Gang setzen kann. In: Geißler, P. & Heisterkamp, G. (Eds.): Psychoanalyse der Lebensbewegungen. Wien: Springer, 555–581.

Ferenczi, S. (2004): Schriften zur Psychoanalyse II. Gießen, Psychosozial.

Ferner, H.; Staubesand, J. (1973): Sobotta/Becher: Atlas der Anatomie des Menschen, Band 3. München: Urban & Schwarzenberg.

Fivaz-Depeursinge, E. & Corboz-Warnery, A. (2001): Das primäre Dreieck. Heidelberg, Carl-Auer. Engl. (1999): The Primary Triangle. New York: Basic Books.

Fivaz-Depeursinge, E., Lavanchy-Scaiola, C., Favez, N. (2010): The Young Infant's Triangular Communication in the Family: Access to Threesome Intersubjectivity? Conceptual Considerations and Case Illustrations. Psychoanalytic Dialogues, 20, 125–140

Gallese, V. (2009): Mirror Neurons, Embodied Simulation, and the Neural Basis of Social Identification. Psychoanalytic Dialogues, 19, 519–536.

Heinrich, V. (1997): Körperliche Phänomene der Gegenübertragung – Therapeuten als Resonanzkörper. Forum der Bioenergetischen Analyse, 1/97, 32–41. Engl. (1999): Physical Phenomena of Countertransference: Therapists as Resonance Body. Bioenergetic Analysis, 10(2), 19–31.

Heinrich-Clauer, V. (2008): Therapeuten als Resonanzkörper: Welche Saiten geraten in Schwingung. In: Heinrich-Clauer, V. (Ed.): Handbuch Bioenergetische Analyse. Gießen: Psychosozial-Verlag, 161–178. Engl. (2011): Therapists as Resonance Body. Which Strings come into Action? In: Heinrich-Clauer, V. (Ed): Handbook Bioenergetic Analysis. Gießen: Psychosozial-Verlag, 149–158.

Herrmann, S. (2012): Nebulöse Mimik. Süddeutsche Zeitung, 277, 18.
Kilian, H. & Köhler, L. (2013): Von der Selbsterhaltung zur Selbstachtung. Gießen: Psychosozial-Verlag.
Kiersky, S. & Beebe, B. (1994): The Reconstruction of Early Nonverbal Relatedness in the Treatment of Difficult Patients: A Special Form of Empathy. Psychoanalytic Dialogues, 4(3): 389–408.
Klitzing, K. von (2002): Frühe Entwicklung im Längsschnitt: Von der Beziehungswelt der Eltern zur Vorstellungswelt des Kindes. Psyche, 56, 863–887.
Krause, R. (1983): Zur Onto- und Phylogenese des Affektsystems und ihrer Beziehungen zu psychischen Störungen. Psyche, 37, 1016–1043.
Kushi, M. (1994): Do-In-Buch: Übungen zur körperlichen und geistigen Entwicklung. Holthausen: Mahajiva.
Lachmann, F. M. (2010): Heimkehren – Going Home. Selbstpsychologie, 39, 86–101.
Lachmann, F. M. (2012): Säuglingsforschung und die Behandlung Erwachsener. Selbstpsychologie, 47, 7–18.
Lewis, R. (2000): Trauma and the Body. Bioenergetic Analysis, 11/2, 61–75.
Lewis, R. (2004): Projective Identification Revisited – Listening with the Limbic System. Bioenergetic Analysis, 14/1, 57–73.
Lewis, R. (2005): The Anatomy of Empathy. Bioenergetic Analysis, 15, 9–31.
Lewis, R. (2008): Der Cephale Schock als Somatisches Verbindungsglied zur Persönlichkeit des Falschen Selbst. In: Heinrich-Clauer, V. (Ed.): Handbuch Bioenergetische Analyse. Gießen: Psychosozial-Verlag, 113–128. Engl.(2011): Cephalic Shock as a Somatic Link to the False Self Personality. In: Heinrich-Clauer, V. (Ed.): Handbook Bioenergetic Analysis. Gießen: Psychosozial-Verlag, 113–127.
Lyons-Ruth, K. (1999): The two-person unconscious: Intersubjective dialogue, enactive relational representation, and the emergence of new forms of relational organization. Psychoanalytic Inquiry, 19, 576–617.
Metzinger, T. (2005): Die Selbstmodell-Theorie der Subjektivität: Eine Kurzdarstellung in sechs Schritten. In: Herrmann, C. S.; Pauen, M.; Rieger, J. W. & Schicktanz, S. (Eds.): Bewusstsein: Philosophie, Neurowissenschaften, Ethik. München: UTB/Fink, 5–32.
Metzinger, T. (2009): Der Ego Tunnel. Berlin Verlag, Berlin. Engl. (2009): The Ego Tunnel. The Science of Mind and the Myth of the Self. New York: Basic Books.
Milch, W. (2001): Lehrbuch der Selbstpsychologie. Stuttgart: Kohlhammer.
Orange, D.; Atwood, G. & Stolorow, R. (1997): Working Intersubjectively: Contextualism in Psychoanalytic Practice. Hillsdale, NJ: The Analytic Press. German: (2001) Intersubjektivität in der Psychoanalyse: Kontextualismus in der psychoanalytischen Praxis. Frankfurt/M.: Brandes & Apsel.
Porges, S. W. (2010): Die Polyvagal-Theorie. Paderborn, Junfermann. Engl. (2011): The Polyvagal Theory. New York: W. W. Norton.
Reich, W. (1972): Die Funktion des Orgasmus. Frankfurt/M.: Fischer. (Orginalausgabe [1942]: The Function of the Orgasm. Orgone Institute Press).
Resnick-Sannes, H. (2002): Psychobiology of Affects: Implications for a Somatic Psychotherapy. Bioenergetic Analysis, 13/1, 111–121.
Resnick-Sannes, H. (2012): Neuroscience, Attachment and Love. Bioenergetic Analysis, 22, 9–28.
Rizzolatti, G.; Fadiga, L.; Fogassi, L., & Gallese, V. (1999): Resonance behaviors and mirror neurons. Archives Italiennes de Biologie, 137, 85–100.
Sander, L. W. (2009): Die Entwicklung des Säuglings, das Werden der Person und die Entstehung

des Bewusstseins. Stuttgart: Klett-Cotta. Engl. (2008): Living Systems, Evolving Consciousness, and the Emerging Person. Hillsdale, NJ: The Analytic Press.
Schore, A. (2005): Erkenntnisfortschritte in Neuropsychoanalyse, Bindungstheorie und Traumaforschung: Implikationen für die Selbstpsychologie. Selbstpsychologie, 6, 395–446. Engl. (2002): Advances in Neuropsychoanalysis, Attachment Theory and Trauma Research: Implications for Self-Psychology. Psychoanalytic Inquiry, 22, 433–484.
Schore, A. (2011): The Right Brain Implicit Self Lies at the Core of Psychoanalysis. Psychoanalytic Dialogues, 21: 55–74.
Schwab, G. (2008) Die schönsten Sagen des klassischen Altertums. Frankfurt/M.: Fischer Tb.
Schwaber, E. A. (2013): Empathie: Eine Form analytischen Zuhörens. Selbstpsychologie, 49, 80–108.
Shapiro, B. (2000): Will Iceberg Sink Titanic. Bioenergetic Analysis, 11/1: 33–42.
Stern, D.N. (1992): Die Lebenserfahrung des Säuglings. Stuttgart: Klett-Cotta. Engl. (1986): The Interpersonal World of the Infants. New York: Basic Books.
Stern, D.N. (2011): Ausdrucksformen der Vitalität. Frankfurt/M., Brandes & Apsel. Engl. (2010): Forms of Vitality: Exploring Dynamic Experience in Psychology, the Arts, Psychotherapy and Development. Oxford: Oxford University Press.
Stern, D.N. et.al. (The Boston Change Study Group) (2012): Veränderungsprozesse. Frankfurt/M.: Brandes & Apsel. Engl: (2010): Change in Psychotherapy. A Unifying Paradigm. New York: W.W. Norton.
Tomasello, M. (2009): Die Ursprünge der menschlichen Kommunikation. Frankfurt/M.: Suhrkamp. Engl. (2008): Origins of human communication. Cambridge, MA: MIT Press.
Tonella, G. (2008): Die Funktionen, Bindungen und Interaktionen des SELBST. In: Heinrich-Clauer, V. (Ed.): Handbuch Bioenergetische Analyse. Gießen: Psychosozial-Verlag, 59–111. Engl. (2011): The Self: Its Functions, its Attachments and its Interactions. In: Heinrich-Clauer, V. (Ed.): Handbook Bioenergetic Analysis. Gießen: Psychosozial-Verlag, 57–112.
Trevarthen, C. (2009): The Intersubjective Psychobiology of Human Meaning: Learning of Culture Depends on Interest for Co-Operative Practical Work and Affection for the Joyful Art of Good Company. Psychoanalytic Dialogues, 19, 507–518.
Winnicott, D.W. (1974: Reifungsprozesse und fördernde Umwelt. Frankfurt/M.: Fischer. Engl. (1990): The Maturational Processes and the Facilitating Environment. London: Karnac.

About the Author

Dr. med. Jörg Clauer, born in 1951; CBT and Faculty Member of IIBA. Biochemist, doctor of psychosomatic medicine and psychotherapy- psychoanalysis (DGPT, DPG, IARPP), psychiatry and psychotherapy, general medicine, rehabilitation. For many years, managerial position in psychosomatic specialist clinics, psychotherapeutic practice since 1999. Lecturer, teaching therapist and supervisor (DGSV) in the field psychotherapy, psychoanalysis, bioenergetic analysis, marriage family and life counseling, coaching, organizational consulting. Various publications in books and journals. Founding member of EfBAP, editorial staff member of the *Forum Bioenergetic Analysis*.

Dr. med. Jörg Clauer
Specialist practice of psychosomatic medicine
and psychotherapy – psychoanalysis.
Krahnstr. 17
49074 Osnabrück
Germany
E-mail: joerg.clauer@osnanet.de

The Alchemy of Ground

John Conger

Abstracts

English

The "Alchemy of Ground" is a personal essay about finding home in nature. Paleo-anthropologists tell us that the mineral structure of the earth and water of our childhood home, written into our bones, identifies our homeland. As one client demonstrates, while culturally we are independent and mobile, we hunger for our body's familiar experience of homeland. More than minerals, the colors of the earth, the guardianship of the trees that think in slow time, the dominance of smell over our artificial sense of time – these draw our bodies back to a communication, deep rhythm and longing for a lost earth, that we split away from and forgot.

Key words: paleo-anthropologists, bones, alchemy, ground, homeland, tree, mineral

German

Die "Alchimie des Grundes" ist ein persönlicher Aufsatz über die Findung einer Heimat in der Natur. Von Paleo-Anthropologen erfahren wir, dass die mineralische Zusammensetzung der Erde und des Wassers der Orte unserer Kindheit unseren Knochen eingeschrieben sei und damit unsere Heimat definiere. Anhand eines Fallbeispiels wird gezeigt, wie wir nach unserer körperlich vertrauten Heimaterfahrung dürsten, während wir kulturell unabhängig und mobil sind. Mehr als die Mineralien, sind es die Farben der Erde, der Schutz der Bäume, die zeitverzögernd denken, die Dominanz unseres Geruchsinns gegenüber unserem artifiziellen Zeitempfinden – die unsere Körper zurück in eine Kommunikation, einen tiefen Rhythmus und eine Sehnsucht nach der verlorenen Erde ziehen, von der wir uns abgespalten und die wir vergessen haben.

French

"L'Alchimie de la Terre" est un essai personnel au sujet du sentiment de se sentir chez soi dans la nature. Les paleo-anthropologues nous apprennent que la structure minérale de la terre et de l'eau de notre enfance, est inscrite dans nos os, et que c'est elle qui détermine le sentiment d'être "chez soi". Comme le démontre un client, alors que, au niveau culturel, nous sommes indépendants et "déplaçables", nous avons un besoin viscéral de cette expérience corporelle d'être "chez soi". En plus des minéraux, les couleurs de la terre, la présence protectrice des arbres qui pensent lentement, les odeurs, bien plus puissantes que notre artificiel découpage du temps, ramènent nos corps au contact du rythme de la profonde nostalgie de la terre perdue; sentiment dont nous nous sommes coupés pour l'oublier.

Spanish

El "Alquimia de la tierra" es un ensayo personal acerca de cómo encontrar el hogar en la naturaleza. Los paleo-antropólogos nos dicen que la estructura mineral de la tierra y el agua del hogar de nuestra infancia escrita en nuestros huesos, identifica a nuestra patria. Tal y como un cliente demuestra, aunque culturalmente somos independientes y móviles, estamos hambrientos por tener nuestra experiencia familiar de la patria en nuestro cuerpo. Más que los minerales, los colores de la tierra, la tutela de los árboles que piensan con lentitud, la dominación del olor sobre nuestro sentido artificial del tiempo nos devuelven a nuestros cuerpos a la comunicación, el ritmo profundo y anhelo de una tierra perdida de la que partimos y a la cual olvidamos.

Portuguese

A "Alquimia do Solo" é um ensaio pessoal sobre a descoberta do lar na natureza. Paleo-antropólogos reportam que a estrutura mineral da terra e da água de nossa terra natal, inscrita em nossos ossos, identifica nossa terra. Como demonstra o caso de um cliente, embora sejamos culturalmente independentes e móveis, ansiamos por nossa experiência corporal familiar da terra natal. Mais do que os minerais, as cores da terra, a guarda das árvores que pensam em câmera lenta, a dominância do cheiro sobre nosso sentido artificial de tempo levam nosso corpo de volta à comunicação, ao ritmo profundo e ao anseio por uma terra perdida, que, em algum momento cortamos fora de nossas vidas e esquecemos.

Essay

Written into the mineral structure of our bones is the signature that locates our homeland. So paleo-anthropologists can determine in the bones they find whether the owner has been born, lived and died in the same place. I'm not sure whether with time the mineral structure of the earth and water of our emotional childhood home will ever be completely washed away by the waters of a new land. As a psychoanalyst, I find the body and the earth so often the forefront of my life and work.

A man told me he never felt at home anywhere. Where he currently lived was the best compromise having been uprooted every few years as a child by his desperate parents, continuously searching for work. He could not locate himself at the deepest levels in a safe place, an essential ground we all need. He spoke to me of his attachments being ripped away throughout childhood, his impotent rage, his invisibility, of emotions unaddressed, so we addressed them school by school, state by state, house by house as good analysts do.

When he was young, my client, Walt, became adept at introducing himself as the new kid to children who had grown up together, performing a rehearsed introduction at every new school, a most compelling first act, even though he, with tears, so desperately longed for a five act play as a child in one place, rather than, as it were, a life of broken attachments, living out of a bus.

His state of homelessness, amid the rock-solid stability of his long established adult life style in one location, continued to haunt him. An analysis could address the unmet emotional residue, but Walt remained a man without a locality, because the pain and failure to ground, to identify himself from somewhere, was visceral, a penetrating sensibility. Initial grounding exercises I'm sorry to say, did not miraculously solve his problem.

It was his body experience that needed to be addressed, the languages in which the body thinks. I told him that the mineral deposits in our bones located us, no matter what, just as certainly as we might track down our forebears through

DNA. But as I inquired about the earthy sensations of places, clearly he was a person of the North. He liked snow, ice skating, the smell of fresh water off of the lake, and of course the sound of loons and he remembered his adolescence in Northern Minnesota where some family remained. We located him just fine.

At last we were talking in the languages of the body, the powerful imprint of a particular kind of black, thick, edgy smells of a bog, of the taste of water and the smell of pine, the sight and feel of peeling white bark of birch trees, of fish and canoes. There were our footprints filling with water stepping out of a boat on a sloping shore. He never liked the south, the heat of Texas and New Mexico.

He just never liked it at all. It was never home there, not like the North.

The man came back another week, if not entirely cured for all time, at least transformed. He knew who he was, where he was from, and who his people were. The North represented a mythology written into his body by the land. It is no accident that throughout the ages the land has been considered the Mother and the Sky, the Father, these mythic parents that seemingly claim us too. What is it like to be brought up in Wyoming with what seems like all that sky? Our body's attachment needs to locate itself in the mother, our ground, because we have lost our place in a culture built on mindless relocations and the loss of a common ethic, community, and the loss of the sky and earth we love, a terrain for some, more certain than family.

Only 100,000 years earlier, we knew so much in the subtle memory and sensibility of the body, so certain and particular. We knew the names of hundreds of plants and trees. Certainly we knew the feel of the sandy soil on our feet as we ran down, 10 years old, on the path overgrown with grasses that bite to the meadows in places thick in mud with the water bringing everything to it. Similarly in our own time here, there was once, at 10 years old, so little to block out under the brilliant omnipotent assault of the sun that claimed us to a particular orb of time, and we, with so little to remember that was not just known.

During September of 2001 returning to Maine for a week from the settled-down homelessness of the West Coast to a summer cottage as remnant of adolescent summers and later visits, my heart thick with the edge of divorce, I felt, to my utter surprise, like I had come home. For so long, displaced, I had dully, as if in a coma, forgotten what I had lost. In Maine, looking out from my house, I saw the lobster boat I remembered being anchored there 50 years ago. Shattoe Island through some trees had not changed nor had the rocks I climbed on when I was so young, at 15. It was the shock of the body remembering, in a flood, what I could not have known as so precious, holding me in something timeless and safe.

I was grounded and unafraid, secure in myself, as if Spirit knew what I most needed and held me there, having me drink full and then drink more for the dark return, to have a refuge within for a while, knowing that I was completely home. Even now those images are somatic script written in for good. After 4 days, I returned to the West coast through the Boston Airport on 9/9/01.

The verbal world has no way to bring us home. Its weapons are useless. We sit in a chair to know it. We have walked, sat and lay down upon this earth for a few million years, our species and our body having won its authority from that ancient lineage. The splitting we have endured being homeless in a world that throws us down, has its cure from the earth and sky if there is such a cure at all. Our local earth has left its location written into every cell, and our body knows when we return.

What memories can match the red earth and the green serpentine that gripped me in the trails near my grandmother's house in Hendersonville, North Carolina, up against the Smoky Mountains, or the feel of warm rain when my brother and I ran to the garage holding up big springy leaves as umbrellas. That was once a home too.

In Art school, I got interested in grinding my own paint. I asked my instructor about it. He told me machines could grind the pigment finer, but he admitted that he had ground his paint for a while. But he had concluded that artists who grind paint generally do not end up painting much.

I found out why a few years later in the cellar of a house my wife and I bought, an old farmhouse in New Jersey, near a school where I taught High School English. In the cellar with light on the marble slab, with dark yellow ochre in powder mixed with linseed oil, or Indian Red in its utter luminescence as I ground it with a pestle, I felt like painting was no longer necessary because no experience of color could be so intense ever again and certainly not in a picture, defused and weakened in shadow.

I was no longer involved with painting but an underlying alchemy intrinsic to earth that so deeply engages our pre-verbal wasteland of body time; so that I might have been paralyzed by the eyes of the unconscious, the eyes of the tiger caught suddenly in the otherwise black coal cellar of night. How can one make a picture after that? One takes space. One spoons the wild color into a metal tube and one seals the end with pliers and one leaves and climbs the stairs. One scrubs off the sticky oil from fingers with the color imbedded at the edge of nail and with the unshakeable smell like a cloud; so in an untimely fashion as if one had forgotten something unbearable, one changes back to normal. I am talking about the sensate, exposed body that we have found too dangerous to adhere to after the forgetfulness of our unprotected childhood.

One of my cats is teaching me about immediacy and the way the body thinks and the limitations of only being grounded in now. I was feeding my favorite wild cat who allows me to pet her, sometimes. I put some cat food on a paper plate and put it down outside on my deck where I always feed her. There are other empty paper plates there because I get tired always cleaning up. The cat followed me excitedly as I put the paper plate down on an older empty plate, my effort to consolidate.

An odd thing happened as she was about to eat. She became confused. She looked furtively about as if wary of attack, and then she backed away without eating. I forgot that late at night, I am visited by raccoons who clean up for me and this cat experienced the raccoons as present because of their fierce smell.

I took the plate off the raccoon's plate and the cat, still hesitant, returned to eat the food uneasily.

This cat was not able to sort out the raccoon of the past with the present moment. I don't blame the cat. The raccoon was absolutely present. Smell is pervasive so as to take possession of a range of time rather than occupy only a passing moment. Smell is like the earth for us that lingers, and collapses memories into one experience.

When I was a child growing up in Staten Island, New York, there was a field I crossed a ways from my house to visit a friend. It turned out returning from my visit, I would climb up into a beech tree with its skin dark and smooth like an elephant. I felt protected and held there. As I got older, I would sometimes walk there at night with the moon in its shifting stages dark or light, and climb up into this tree's branches as if visiting an old friend, an earthly grandparent. Years later, returning from college, I walked late at night to the field only to find it had been co-opted by tract homes. I found my beech tree trapped in the close right angle of a house. As quietly as I could, and every sound echoed, I climbed that tree defiantly and stayed there for a while, for a moment safe, heartbroken by inexorable time.

In Berkeley, in my back yard is a live oak sustained in life for a few hundred years by a nearby stream. My house was built in 1913, but the tree is so much older. My house represents a constructed thought that has held its own through the years with some decks added. The redwoods that border my property have a design that says "Grow tall and spread now."

In remarkable contrast the live oak has extended its limbs out relatively parallel to the ground for 30 or 40 feet held only by a thick double trunk. From one massive trunk another huge branch reaches up and out twenty feet at a 45-degree angle branching out 8 or 9 times into repeated branches, finally resorting to leaves; and there are squirrels and birds and many limbs to accommodate them. I sit here once more attempting to draw the life of this bewildering tree so much older than me, so visually complex, so remarkably successful at life in the open. I am struck by how this tree thinks in its own slow time. And how fortunate I am to be in the company of my brilliant elders. My indoor/outdoor personal cat, barely two years old, sprawls calm and perfectly attuned on the deck at my feet.

What dominates me is this Live Oak, as incomprehensible as a small god. If I had a machine that could bring all our being into the same rhythmic breath, just a momentary gathering for a chat, there is nothing that I could learn more powerful than this tree holding ground thinking as only an old tree can think stretched out, breathing in the water so deep down in an earth that has its own pulse, an earth that has written its signature of some place else, its time and place in the cell structure of my bones. In my evolutionary being that I could not have reached but has found me, for a moment in an unconstructed space without intent, through what I assume is the extended grace of this remarkable tree and the earth that owns me, I feel, displaced as I am, not so much at home as included and for the moment, at peace.

A car stopped in my driveway, a day ago. A man with his aging mother in her late 80's and his wife, had returned to his childhood home to look at it from the outside, so I invited them in to walk around. They were profoundly grateful, having passed the house now and again not daring to bother the owner with their desire to walk on the same ground and look out the windows, or step onto the deck upstairs. Walking through the house, the man was possessed. This was my room. That was my brother's room. Look, there's the same bathroom, the same tile. Over there used to be a door to the kitchen. His mother said she always missed the views of the Bay. Where she lived now, there were no views.

In a powerful return like Odysseus to Ithaca, this man savored the native earth that infused his distinct composition and held the memories that grounded him in time. Outside, the man told me his father had planted the towering redwoods. But the Live Oak amazed him, in particular the great long branches reaching toward the house. They had not grown out that way 40 years ago. He and his brother had climbed that tree and swung on ropes from it and had a metal swing set where these branches now reached. He promised to send me pictures of the house of over forty years ago, when he was an adolescent. I have a picture of the house much earlier when it was only one of two houses built on this hill.

At least I study and teach in a branch of psychology that includes the evolutionary body in its rhythm and voice, because the body holds images that the facile mind cannot access. My mind thinks it is ready for anything, any bad news certainly. My immediate time-driven mind is rather shocked when an image appears that from my point of view, should have showed up for me many years ago.

But my body thinks more like a tree. It takes forty years to grow a long impossible limb far out, sustained in what appears on the outside to be unsustainable, so much weight with so little direct support. Some of our illnesses take a lifetime of thought, acting through the limbs. And so our body of particular earth holds something with no urgency unless met in its own language and on its own irreducible terms.

About the Author

Dr. John Conger is a psychologist, a psychoanalyst, an IIBA faculty member and an Episcopal Priest. He is a core faculty member at Meridian University. He has a private practice in Kensington, Ca. He is the author of *Jung and Reich: the Body as Shadow, and The Body In Recovery: Somatic Psychotherapy and the Self.* He is presently writing a third book about Bioenergetics and the self.

Dr. John Conger
E-mail: johncongerphd@gmail.com

Searching for Active Factors in Diverse Approaches to Psychotherapy – Types of Intervention and Temporal Aspects

Brief Research Report[1]

Margit Koemeda-Lutz, Aureliano Crameri, Peter Schulthess, Agnes von Wyl & Volker Tschuschke

Abstracts

English

This paper is a synopsis of scientific research on treatment effectiveness of ten varying approaches to psychotherapy. Different types of psychotherapy justify their existence by the basic assumption that therapeutic change is effectuated by specific concepts, attitudes and interventional techniques. In comparative psychotherapy research, for many years, studies have quantified outcome differences (see e.g. Lambert, 2013), and only very few have closely examined the process of treatment. The study reported here was part of a larger multi-center naturalistic process-outcome study (pre-post-follow-up, see e.g. von Wyl et al., 2013; Crameri et al., 2015; Tschuschke et al., 2015), named PAP-S, which included 362 patients from 81 therapists. The synopsis includes methods as well as results and discussion.

Key words: naturalistic process outcome study, treatment effectiveness research, synopsis, psychotherapy approaches

German

Im Rahmen einer Studie zur Wirksamkeit von zehn unterschiedlichen Therapiemethoden berichtet dieser Beitrag über eine vergleichende Untersuchung

1 Brief Paper Presentation at the 8th European Conference on Psychotherapy Research, September 24th–26th, Klagenfurt, Austria.

von verbalem Therapeutenverhalten in konkreten Sitzungen. Unterschiedliche Therapiemethoden rechtfertigen ihre Existenz mit der Grundannahme, dass therapeutische Veränderung durch spezifische Konzepte, Haltungen und Interventionstechniken bewirkt werde. In der vergleichenden Psychotherapieforschung wurden über Jahre Ergebnisunterschiede quantifiziert, nur sehr wenige Studien haben den Behandlungsprozess näher untersucht. Die hier berichteten Ergebnisse basieren auf Daten aus einer naturalistischen, multizentrischen Prozess-Ergebnisuntersuchung (prä, post und katamnestisch), PAP-S, die 362 Patient/innen von 81 Therapeut/innen einschloss. Der Beitrag beschreibt die verwendeten Methoden, berichtet Ergebnisse und diskutiert sie.

French

Faisant partie d'une étude plus large portant sur l'efficacité de dix approches différentes à la psychothérapie, cet article fait état d'une recherche comparative s'intéressant au comportement à l'intérieur d'une séance. Différents types de psychothérapies justifient leur existence en tenant pour acquis que le changement au plan thérapeutique s'explique à partir de concepts, d'attitudes et de techniques d'intervention. Dans de domaine de la recherche comparative en psychothérapie, et ce pendant plusieurs années, les études ont cherché à quantifier les différences en termes de résultats et très peu d'entre elles ont examiné de près le processus de traitement en soi. Les résultats dont il est fait mention ici se fondent sur des données provenant d'une étude multi-centre sur l'impact du processus, menée dans le contexte d'un environnement naturel (en angl. *a multi-center naturalistic process-outcome study*) (pré-post follow-up), appelée PAP-S. Elle inclut 362 patients suivis par 81 thérapeutes. L'article présente la méthodologie utilisée, les résultats ainsi qu'une discussion de ceux-ci.

Spanish

Como parte de un estudio más amplio sobre la eficacia de los diez enfoques diferentes en la psicoterapia, este ensayo informa sobre una investigación comparativa del comportamiento en la sesión terapéutica. Diferentes tipos de psicoterapia justifican su existencia basado en el supuesto de que el cambio terapéutico se efectúa por determinados conceptos, actitudes y técnicas de intervención. Durante muchos años, en la investigación comparativa de la psicoterapia los estudios han cuantificado las diferencias de resultado y sólo muy pocos han examinado muy de cerca el proceso del tratamiento. Los resultados que aquí se reportan se basan en los datos de un estudio de proceso-resultado multicentro naturalista (pre-post-seguimiento), llamados PAP-S, en el que participaron 362 pacientes de 81 terapeutas. El documento incluye métodos, así como resultados y discusiones.

Portuguese

Sendo parte de um estudo mais amplo sobre a efetividade de dez abordagens diferentes de psicoterapia, este artigo relata uma investigação comparativa do comportamento terapêutico dentro de uma sessão. Diferentes tipos de psicoterapia baseiam sua existência na suposição básica de que a transformação terapêutica ocorre através de conceitos, atitudes e técnicas de intervenção específicos. Durante um longo tempo, estudos de pesquisa comparativa de psicoterapias têm apontado diferenças quantitativas nos resultados, mas somente muito poucas têm examinado, mais atentamente, o processo de tratamento. Os resultados aqui relatados se baseiam em dados originados num processo naturalista multicentrado de um estudo de resultados (follow up pré e pós), denominado PAP-S, do qual participaram 362 pacientes de 81 terapeutas. O artigo inclui métodos, resultados e discussão.

1. Introduction

Interventional behaviour of psychotherapists is usually based on theoretical concepts from specific psychotherapeutic approaches and technical recommendations derived thereof. They imply anthropological assumptions, premises about health and health disorders, as well as theories of change.

Different types of psychotherapy justify their existence by the basic assumption that therapeutic change is effectuated by specific concepts, attitudes and interventional techniques. In comparative psychotherapy research, for many years, studies have quantified outcome differences (see e.g. Lambert, 2013), and only very few have closely examined the process of treatment. The majority of research so far has failed to prove that approaches under examination actually implemented techniques which they claim to be specific to their type of psychotherapy (see e.g. Perepletchikova et al., 2007).

The study which is reported here was part of a larger multi-center naturalistic process-outcome study (pre-post-follow-up, see e.g. von Wyl et al., 2013; Crameri et al., 2015; Tschuschke et al., 2015), named PAP-S, which included 362 patients from 81 therapists and ten different types of psychotherapy. Patients were from a wide and heterogeneous diagnostic range. Diagnoses (SKID (First et al., 2012), OPD (2001), Global Assessment Functioning Scale (APA, 1989), and Axes I, II, and V, DSM-IV (APA, 1994) were assessed by external experts.

Type of psychotherapy	Participating institutes	Founders	Main approach
Analytical Psychology	C. G. Jung Institute, ISAP, SGAP	C. G. Jung	Psychodynamic
Art and Expression Oriented Therapy	Europäische Gesellschaft für Interdisziplinäre Studien (EGIS)	P .J. Knill	Integrative
Bioenergetic Analysis	Schweiz.Gesellschaft für Bioenergetische Analyse und Therapie (SGBAT, DÖK)	A. Lowen	Body oriented, psychodynamic
Existential Analysis and Logotherapy	Institut für Logotherapie und Existenzanalyse (ILE, GES)	V. E. Frankl	Humanistic
Gestalt Therapy	Schweizerischer Verein für Gestalttherapie (SVG)	F. Perls	Humanistic
Integrative Body Psychotherapy	Integrative Body Psychotherapy (IBP)	J. L. Rosenberg	Body oriented, integrative
Process Oriented Psychotherapy	Institut für Prozessarbeit (IPA)	A. Mindell	Psychodynamic
Psychoanalysis (PSZ)	Psychoanalytisches Seminar Zürich (PSZ)	S. Freud	Psychodynamic
Transactional Analysis	Schweizerische Gesellschaft für Transaktionsanalyse (SGTA, ASAT)	E. Berne	Humanistic

Table 1. Types of Psychotherapy Investigated

In the present study we investigated therapists' interventional behaviour, who claimed to be affiliated with one of eight different types of psychotherapy: Psychoanalysis (Freud, 1895–1940), Art and Expression Oriented Psychotherapy (Knill et al., 1995), Bioenergetic Analysis (Lowen, 1958), Existential Analysis and Logotherapy (Frankl, 1956–1999), Gestalt Therapy (Perls et al., 1951), Integrative Body Psychotherapy (Rosenberg et al., 1996), Process Oriented Psychotherapy (Mindell, 1998), and Transactional Analysis (Berne, 1961).

Our aims were twofold: First, to assess how frequently therapists actually employed interventions specific to their own approach under naturalistic conditions, versus how frequently they employed interventions specific to other approaches or interventions that were common across all approaches. Would therapists' affiliation with a certain type of psychotherapy predict their interventional behaviour? In case it didn't, which other factors would? Secondly, we headed for identifying types of intervention used by therapists that systematically engendered lengthy (> 120 seconds) interaction units between therapist and patient. If such types of intervention existed, we hypothesized, they might involve more complex and "deeper" levels of processing in patients, possibly indicating processes of change. Unfortunately, we found only very few other studies investigating temporal aspects of therapist-patient interactions (Duncan, 1972; Rochet-Caplan & Fuchs, 2014; Langs & Badalamenti, 1990; Badalamenti & Langs, 1991).

2. Method

The data presented here are based on two studies (Koemeda-Lutz et al., 2016 a in print; 2016 b, in print). This report focusses on the second one.

2.1. Sample

Out of a total of 13'351 sessions, audio-recorded between 2007 and 2013, a sample of 422 sessions from 92 patients and 42 therapists was drawn. Patients were comparable to other outcome studies, concerning diagnoses, sex and age, as well as socioeconomic data (von Wyl et al., 2013).

As to be expected in a naturalistic study we fell short of reaching an ideal distribution of variables: ideal would have been an equal number of therapists representing each type of psychotherapy, 3 patients from each therapist, and 3 sessions per patient, one from the beginning, one from the middle and one from the end of therapy.

Table 2 shows the actual distribution falling short of our stratification goals – due to patient and therapist drop-outs, recordings of poor acoustic quality etc.

2.2. Variables

Therapeutic interventions were coded according to a rating manual (PAP-S-RM, Tschuschke et al., 2014) by 5 raters, students of psychology, who were not trained

type of psychotherapy	**Psychoanalyis/Analytical Psychology**					
founders	S. Freud, C.G. Jung					
therapist code	A				B	C
patient code	a1	a2	a3	a4	b1	c1
no.analyzed sessions	3	3	3	10	3	3

type of psychotherapy	**Existential Analysis and Logotherapy**			
founders	V.Frankl			
therapist code	K	L		M
patient code	k1	l1	l2	m1
no.analyzed sessions	4	3	3	3

type of psychotherapy	**Gestalt Therapy**											
founders	F. Perls											
therapist code	D					E		F	G	H	I	J
patient code	d1	d2	d3	d4	d5	e1	e2	f1	g1	h1	i1	j1
no.analyzed sessions	14	9	3	3	3	3	3	15	3	3	3	3

type of psychotherapy	**Transactional Analysis**											
founders	E.Berne											
therapist code	N	O	P		Q				R			
patient code	n1	o1	p1	p2	q1	q2	q3	q4	r1	r2	r3	r4
no.analyzed sessions	3	3	13	15	3	3	3	3	3	3	3	3

type of psychotherapy	**Bioenergetic Analysis**									
founders	A. Lowen									
therapist code	S			T	U		V	W		X
patient code	s1	s2	s3	t1	u1	u2	v1	w1	w2	x1
no.analyzed sessions	19	3	4	3	3	3	5	3	3	3

type of psychotherapy	**Process Oriented Psychotherapy**																					
founders	A. Mindell																					
therapist code	Y				Z				AA	AB			AC					AD	AE			
patient code	y1	y2	y3	y4	z1	z2	z3	z4	aa1	ab1	ab2	ab3	ac1	ac2	ac3	ac4	ac5	ad1	ae1	ae2	ae3	ae4
no.analyzed sessions	11	17	3	3	3	3	3	3	3	3	4	3	3	3	3	3	16	3	3	3	3	3

type of psychotherapy	**Art and Expression Oriented Therapy**							
founders	P.J.Knill & B.H.Nienhaus							
therapist code	AN			AO			AP	
patient code	an1	an2	an3	ao1	ao2	ao3	ap1	ap2
no.analyzed sessions	3	3	3	3	3	15	3	3

type of psychotherapy	**Integrative Body Psychotherapy**																		total
founders	J.L. Rosenberg																		
therapist code	AF				AG	AH		AI		AJ				AK		AL		AM	42
patient code	af1	af2	af3	af4	ag1	ah1	ah2	ai1	ai2	aj1	aj2	aj3	aj4	ak1	ak2	al1	al2	am1	92
no.analyzed sessions	3	3	3	2	3	3	3	3	3	3	3	3	3	3	3	3	16	11	422

4 nested factors: type of psychotherapy, therapist, patient, session

Table 2. Sample

in any type of psychotherapy and who were blind with respect to therapists' affiliations as well as to the attribution of types of intervention to types of psychotherapy. Table 3 gives an example of one such intervention category *Focus on emotional experiencing*.

Category 8: Focus on emotional experiencing
Definition
Therapist's questions aim at exploring patient's quality of experiencing, sensations, and feelings. Beliefs, appraisals, explanations or assumptions are not areas of inquiry. Therapist guides patient to focus on her/his present experiencing, sensations, and feelings (to which the patient supposedly has conscious access).
Operationalization
Therapist
– asks about present state of being
– asks about present quality of experiencing
– clarifies on an emotional level
Differentiation
(19) shifting focus of attention to present emotion, of which the patient supposedly is unconscious
(55) clarifying inquiry: exploration of facts, events, cognitions, not emotions
Examples
1) How do you experience this? How do you feel about it?
2) You explained to me the way this happened and why Mr. F. did what he did, but I would like to know how you feel about it.

Table 3. Intervention Category from Rating Manual (Tschuschke et al., 2014)

For each therapist speech turn, coders assigned one of 100 interventions identified in the Rating Manual as a common intervention, an approach-specific intervention, or a specific intervention from other approaches.

Table 4 presents intervention categories which proponents from Psychoanalysis and from Bioenergetic Analysis, respectively, claimed to be specific to their approach. As can be seen, some categories were claimed by both types of psychotherapy as specific to their approach (specific but not unique): *transference, countertransference* and *interpretation*.

Psychoanalysis (PSZ)
1. Confronting defenses
11. Working on preconscious material
15. Encouraging free associations
27. Interpretation (SGBAT)
29. Working through painful insights, irretrievable losses, etc.
40. Countertransference (C.G. Jung, BAT)
55. Clarifying inquiry / exploration (C, GES)
60. Confrontation
90. Discussing transference (C.G. Jung, BAT)
Bioenergetic Analysis (SGBAT, DÖK)
2. Affect regulation (SVG)
17. Breath work (IBP)
27. Interpretation (PSA)
35. Experimenting with novel behavior (SVG, TA, CBT)
40. Countertransference (C.G. Jung, PSA)
56. Promoting somatic experiencing SVG, IBP)
57. Focusing on physical impulses (SVG, IBP)
58. Teaching a body exercise
61. Congruence, sensing incongruence (SVG, Rogerian)

Table 4. Approach Specific Interventions (approaches also claiming them as specific in brackets)

The interrater reliability on a single intervention basis was assessed for 80 sessions. Interventions were coded independently by two students. This resulted in a Kappa coefficient of 0.68 (Cohen, 1988), which according to Landis and Koch (1977, p. 165) can be qualified as "substantial strength of agreement."

For the investigation of temporal aspects the onset of therapists' utterances, consisting of at least one complete sentence was recorded. Therapists' utterances in the investigated sample of 422 sessions amounted to a total of N = 18'542 interventions. The duration of intervals from the onset of one intervention to the next was computed (= 1 interaction unit). For simplicity's sake therapists' utterances were called "interventions" and patients' utterances "reactions." From a systemic point of view this could, of course, be reversed.

3. Results

3.1. Categorial Aspects: Descriptive

External raters identified on average 43 interventions and 15 different types of intervention per session. Only 14% of all interventions were specific to therapists' own type of psychotherapy. 66% were common and 20% were interventions specific to other types of psychotherapy. The number of interventions (8 to 173) and their specificity (0 to 57% and 2 to 78%) varied considerably from session to session. A little more than one third of all interventions were specific (34%), 1.4 times as many from other approaches than from therapists' own. Figure 1 reveals that Process-Oriented Psychotherapists used least and Psychoanalytic Therapists the most specific interventions. This result will be commented on in the discussion.

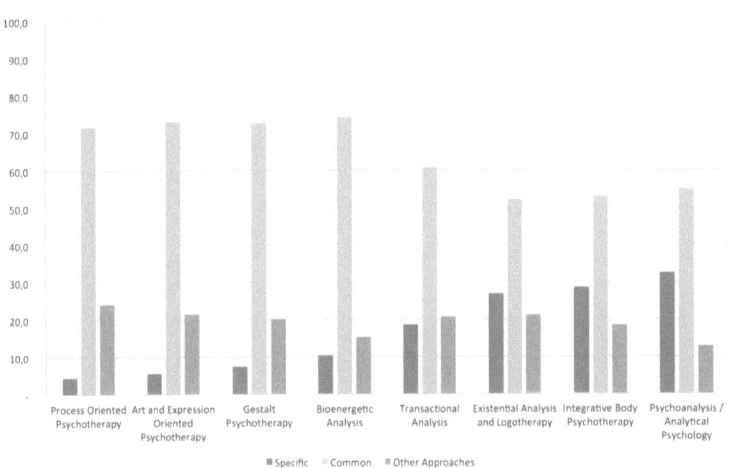

Figure 1. Types of intervention, mean frequences (%)

In all types of psychotherapy investigated, three categories of intervention played a dominant role. They were clarifying inquiry, advice/information, and support (in total 37%, see table 5, left column). All three are common categories, shared by a variety of types of psychotherapy. The total number of common, approach-specific, and specific to other approaches interventions across all of the sessions were tallied and a one-way ANOVA was conducted to determine if therapists' use of common and approach-specific interventions differed according to their self-identified approach.

10 most frequently applied interventions	%	10 interventions filling most of the time, patients' responses included	time	% time	10 interventions succeeded by longest intervals to next intervention (f ≥ 10)	average duration	%
55: clarifying inquiry / exploration	15,02	55: clarifying inquiry / exploration	74:21:59	21,71	62: activating aesthetic responsibility (EGIS)	00:04:00	0,2 *
52: providing information / giving advice	11,26	52: providing information / giving advice	45:44:40	13,35	33: teaching relaxation technique (VT, IBP)	00:03:53	0,1 *
46: providing support	10,88	46: providing support	30:27:38	8,89	58: teaching a body exercise (SGBAT)	00:02:32	0,5 *
30: promoting insight	7,91	30: promoting insight	25:44:29	7,51	14: stimulating creativity (SGAP, EGIS)	00:02:17	0,1 *
31: empathy	6,12	31: empathy	16:32:31	4,83	25: teaching about agency (character defenses) (IBP)	00:02:01	0,5 *
60: confrontation (PSZ)	4,81 *	60: confrontation (PSZ)	12:11:06	3,56 *	77: teaching or suggesting mental health tools (IBP)	00:01:52	0,1 *
19. directing attention to unconscious emotions	3,84	27: interpretation(PSZ)	10:05:51	2,95 *	95: perceptual sensitization (EGIS)	00:01:49	0,4 *
27: interpretation(PSZ)	3,68 *	19. directing attention to unconscious emotions	9:58:52	2,91	11: working on preconscious material (PSZ)	00:01:43	0,4 *
8: emotional experiencing	3,34	56: somatic experiencing (BAT, SVG, IBP)	9:19:03	2,72 *	67: finding meaning while creating (EGIS)	00:01:41	0,2 *
56: somatic experiencing (BAT, SVG, IBP)	2,25 *	8: emotional experiencing	8:58:39	2,62	5: taking anamnestic information	00:01:37	1,8
% of all interventions	69,11	% of total session time		71,06	% of total session time		4,30

* specific interventions (abbreviations for types of psychotherapy in parentheses)

Psychoanalysis/Analytical Psychology (PSZ, SGAP, ISAP)
Existential Analysis and Logotherapy (GES)
Gestalt Therapy (SVG)
Transactional Analysis (SGTA/ASAT)
Bioenergetic Analysis (SGBAT, DÖK)
Process Oriented Psychotherapy (IPA)
Art and Expression Oriented Therapy (EGIS)
Integrative Body Psychotherapy (IBP)

Table 5. The 10 Most Frequently Applied, the 10 Most Time Consuming, and the 10 Types of Interventions Followed by Intervals of On-Average Longest Duration (N = 422 sessions)

Results showed that therapists' professed adherence notwithstanding, the majority of interventions used were common to all approaches, while the interventions used least were those specific to therapists' self-identified approach (see figure 1).

3.2. Categorial Aspects: Predictive

Multilevel Modelling

To answer the question of which factors predict the use of different types of intervention,

No.	Intervention category	Error probabilities and levels of significance					
		approach	p	therapist	p	patient	p
1	Confronting defenses (PSA)	1,0000		0,6575		0,0207	*
5	Taking history information (C)	0,9998		0,9994		0,0000	***
8	Emotional experiencing (C)	0,9993		0,1470		0,0003	***
11	Working on preconscious material (PSA)	1,0000		0,9999		0,0000	***
12	Using humor (C)	0,9999		0,0003		0,0000	***
19	Directing attention to unconscious emotions (C, SVG)	0,9999		0,0226	*	0,0000	***
21	Exploration of behavioral patterns and beliefs (C, SVG, TA)	0,9998		0,4652		0,0012	**
22	Unconditional positive regard (Rogerian)	0,9986		0,9998		0,0000	***
24	Biographical work (C, IBP, GES)	0,6724		0,2774		0,0038	**
27	Interpretation (PSA, SGBAT)	0,9999		0,0163	*	0,0000	***
30	Promoting insight into the necessity of behavior change (C, GES)	0,9267		0,1936		0,0000	***
31	Empathy (C, Rogerian)	0,8266		0,0801		0,0000	***
32	Working with boundaries, gradients of distance (IBP)	0,0277	*	0,3176		0,0000	***
40	Countertransference (C.G. Jung, PSA, SGBAT)	0,9978		0,9999		0,0000	***

Continued on next page

No.	Intervention category	Error probabilities and levels of significance					
		approach	p	therapist	p	patient	p
42	Purposeful frustration (SVG)	0,3587		0,8835		0,1225	
46	Providing support (C, TA)	1,0000		0,0000	***	0,0000	***
52	Providing information / giving advice (C, IBP)	0,6859		0,0090	**	0,0000	***
55	Clarifying inquiry / exploration (C, GES, PSA)	0,4627		0,0007	***	0,0000	***
60	Confrontation (PSA)	0,9998		0,3444		0,0000	***
65	Working with metaphor (systemic)	1,0000		1,0000		0,0833	
69	Positive reinforcement (CBT	0,9996		0,1527		0,0000	***
72	Reframing (systemic)	0,9229		0,0239	*	0,0001	***
75	Resource activation (C, GES)	1,0000		0,4486		0,0109	*
78	Self-disclosure by the therapist (C)	0,3146		0,0668		0,0000	***
80	Creating meaning (SGAP, ISAP, C. G Jung Institute)	0,9989		0,9027		0,0017	**
85	Addressing symptoms (C)	1,0000		0,7267		0,0000	***
87	Changing the topic (C)	0,9999		1,0000		0,0323	*
88	Referring to the therapy contract (C, TA)	1,0000		0,9999		0,0000	***
89	Addressing therapy goals (C, TA)	1,0000		0,0001	***	0,0075	**

** = $p < 0.05$; ** = $p < 0.01$; *** = $p < 0.001$*

Art and Expression Oriented Therapy (EGIS), Bioenergetic Analysis (SGBAT), Cognitive Behavior Therapy (CBT), Existential Analysis and Logotherapy (GES), Gestalt Therapy (SVG), Integrative Body Psychotherapy (IBP), Process Oriented Psychotherapy (IPA), Psychoanalysis/Analytical Psychology (PSZ, SGAP, ISAP, C. G. Jung Institute), Transactional Analysis (SGTA/ASAT)

Table 6. Comparison of Four Poisson Regression Models

4 multilevel regression models (see Bryk and Raudenbush, 1992) were computed, excluding intervention categories that were used in less than 10% of all sessions. One model included 3 (approach, therapist, patient), the other 3 models 2 random effects each (therapist, patient), (approach, patient), (approach therapist). The latter were compared with the first model including 3 factors, using the likelihood ratio test. Except for one single intervention category the use of interventions varied independently of therapists' affiliation to certain types of

psychotherapy. The factor *therapist* predicted the variability of intervention frequencies for 7 intervention categories. The factor *patient* was most informative for predicting the variability of intervention type frequencies. Table 6 presents the pertaining error probabilities.

3.3. Temporal Aspects: Descriptive

The same 10 intervention categories as the 10 most frequently used (69%) also filled 71% of the total session time investigated (see table 5, left and middle columns). At the same time we observed that intervals between interventions (the duration of intervention units) varied considerably within and across sessions.

In figure 2 the onsets of interventions in three different sessions are represented by horizontal bars along the continuum of time (y-axis).

Medians of interval durations for each type of intervention were computed. Categories having been employed less than 50 times in all sessions under study were excluded.

In a one-way analysis of variance types of intervention were not predictive for interval duration. But intervention categories could be arranged according to average interval duration following their use in descending order.

Especially specific intervention categories involved interactional units of longest durations. We created a time interval x intervention contingency table and computed chi-square values to determine which interventions led to lengthy interactions more frequently than would be expected by chance. Results identified the 10 interventions most likely to set off interaction units lasting longer than 120 seconds (see table 5, right column).

4. Discussion

Common intervention techniques are employed twice as often as compared to intervention categories specific to certain types of psychotherapy, roughly one and a half as many from other as from therapists' own type of psychotherapy, which replicates findings by Lambert (1992). Eclecticism was clearly present. Therapists' affiliation with different types of psychotherapy did not predict their interventional behaviour. Therapists seem to have developed personal styles which make their use of some types of intervention more likely than others. The factor

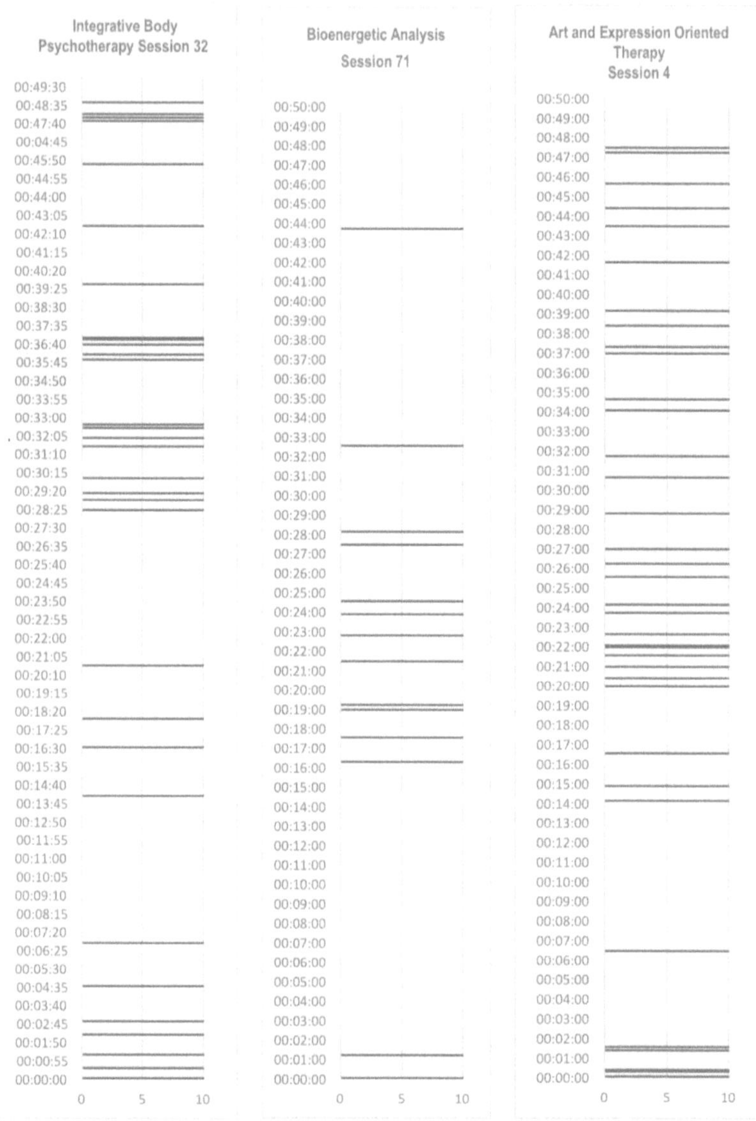

Figure 2. Varying pace of therapists' interventional behavior in different sessions

patient however best predicted which types of intervention were employed, thus complying with Lambert's (2013) and Norcross and Wampold's (2011) request that therapists should try to match "techniques to client dispositions, personality traits and other diagnostic differences."

Proponents of some approaches claimed interventions as specific to their type of psychotherapy, whereas in fact these were shared by all types investigated in our study (e.g., Psychoanalysis and Logotherapy claimed *clarifying inquiry*, Transactional Analysis claimed *support,* and Integrative Body Psychotherapy claimed *providing information/giving advice* as interventions specific to their approach. These four approaches have higher scores of "specific" interventions than the rest. In this light, differences in specificity between approaches seem to be largely due to different conceptualizations of specificity in different types of psychotherapy.

What cannot be observed are the concepts and strategies that therapists have in mind while they are interacting with their patients. Possibly these are relevant all the same. And from an external perspective, therapists' concept orientation may have been underestimated. Common interventions may have prepared the ground for the attainment of type of psychotherapy-specific goals.

In almost all sessions there were sections in which the pace of patient-therapist interactions slowed down. Interventions that were followed by exceptionally long intervals to the next intervention were frequently specific interventions.

Interventions that mostly tended to slow down the pace of therapists' interventional behavior were interventions specific to certain types of psychotherapy. Although their prevalence was not high, we think that these are worth investigating more closely. We suspect that prolonged interactional units could be indicative of change coming about in patients' habitual patterns. Processing emotional irritation (Achtziger et al., 2014) or tasks of higher complexity take more time, as e.g. Sternberg (1975), Kintsch (1982), or Roth (1994) have pointed out. Verbatim transcripts done from our material also point into this direction.

The prevalence of 34% of specific interventions from different approaches, although eclectically applied, does not advise discarding the variety of different types of psychotherapy existing at present. On the contrary, the existing wealth of concepts and techniques should be acknowledged, carefully investigated, and integrated in therapeutic practice. It would probably be wise to acknowledge the role of common factors in effective treatments while also considering the usefulness of specific interventions from approaches that are not yet established as evidence-based.

References

Achtziger, A., Gollwitzer, P.M., Bergius, R. & Schmalt, H.-D. (2014). Motiv. In Wirtz, M.A. (Eds.), *Dorsch. Lexikon der Psychologie.* 17. Auflage (pp. 1113–1116). Bern: Huber.

American Psychiatric Association. (1989). Global Assessment of Functioning Scale. *Diagnostische Kriterien und Differentialdiagnosen des diagnostischen und statistischen Manuals psychischer Störungen DSM-III-R.* Weinheim: Beltz.

American Psychiatric Association. (1994) Diagnostic and Statistical Manual of Mental Disorders DSM-IV. Washington D.C.

Badalamenti, A.F. & Langs, R.J. (1991). An empirical investigation of human dyadic systems in the time and frequency domains. *Journal of Behavioral Science, 36(2), pp. 100–114.* doi:10.1002/bs.3830360204

Berne, E. (1961). *Transactional Analysis in psychotherapy: A systematic individual and social psychiatry.* New York, NY: Grove Press.

Bryk, A. & Raudenbush, S.W. (1992). *Hierarchical linear models: Applications and data analysis methods.* Thousand Oaks, CA: Sage.

Cohen, J. (1988). *Statistical power analysis for the behavioral sciences* (2nd ed.). Hillsdale, NJ: Lawrence Erlbaum.

Crameri, A., von Wyl, A., Koemeda-Lutz, M., Tschuschke, V., & Schulthess, P. (2015). Sensitivity analysis in multiple imputation in effectiveness studies of psychotherapy. *Frontiers in Psychology;* doi:10.3389/fpsyg.2015.01042

Duncan, S. (1972). Some signals and rules for taking speaking turns in conversations. *Journal of Personality and Social Psychology, 23(2), pp. 283–292.* doi:10.1037/h0033031

First, M.B., Spitzer, R.L., Giblon, M. & Williams, J.B.W. (2012). *Structured Clinical Interview for DSM-IV (SCID I and II).* books.google.com (In German: Wittchen, H.U., Zaudig, M. & Fydrich, T. (1997). *Strukturiertes Klinisches Interview für DSM-IV.* Göttingen, Germany: Hogrefe. And: Saß, H., Wittchen, H.U., & Zaudig, M. (2003). *Diagnostisches und Statistisches Manual Psychischer Störungen (DSM-IV-TR)* [Diagnostic and statistical manual of mental disorders (DSM-IV-TR)]. Göttingen, Germany: Hogrefe.

Frankl, V.E. (1956–1999). *Theorie und Therapie der Neurosen: Einführung in die Logotherapie und Existenzanalyse* [Theory and therapy of neuroses: Introduction to logotherapy and existential analysis]. Munich: Ernst Reinhardt.

Freud, S. (1895–1940). *Gesammelte Werke [Collected Works]:* Vols. 1–17. Frankfurt: S. Fischer.

Hautzinger, M., Keller, F. & Kühne, C. (2006). *BDI-II: Beck Depressionsinventar.* Frankfurt, Germany: Harcourt Test Services.

Jung, C.G. (2000). *Gesammelte Werke [Collected Works]:* Vols. 1–20. Ostfildern, Germany: Patmos.

Kintsch, W. (1982). *Gedächtnis und Kognition* [Memory and cognition]. Berlin, Germany: Springer.

Knill, P.J., Nienhaus Barba, H. & Fuchs, M. (1995). *Minstrels of Soul: Intermodal expressive therapy.* Toronto, Canada: EGS-Press.

Koemeda-Lutz, M., Crameri, A., Tschuschke, V., Schulthess, P., & von Wyl, A. (2016 a, in print) Therapists' interventions in different psychotherapy approaches Category and temporal aspects. *International Body Psychotherapy Journal*

Koemeda-Lutz, M., Crameri, A., Schulthess, P., von Wyl, A., & Tschuschke, V. (in print) Specificity and Pace Variability of Therapists' Interventions under Naturalistic Conditions. *International Journal for Psychotherapy*

Lambert, M. J. (1992). Psychotherapy outcome research: Implications for integrative and eclectic therapists. In J. C. Norcross & M. R. Goldfried (Eds.), *Handbook of psychotherapy integration* (pp. 94–129). New York, NY: Basic Books.

Lambert, M.J. (Eds.). (2013). The efficacy and effectiveness of psychotherapy. In M.J. Lambert (Ed.), *Bergin and Garfield's Handbook of Psychotherapy and Behavior Change* (6th ed.), (pp. 169–218). Hoboken, NJ: John Wiley & Sons.

Landis, J. R. & Koch, G. G. (1977). The measurement of observer agreement for categorical data. *Biometrics, 33(1), pp. 159–174.* doi:10.2307/2529310

Langs, R. J. & Badalamenti, A. F. (1990). Stochastic analysis of the duration of the speaker role in psychotherapy. *Perceptual Motor Skills, 70, pp. 675–689.* doi:10.2466/pms.1990.70.2.675

Lowen, A. (1958). *The Language of the Body.* New York: Prentice Hall.

Mindell, A. (1998). *Dreambody.* Portland, OR: Lao Tse Press.

Norcross, J. C., & Wampold, B. E. (2011). What works for whom: Tailoring psychotherapy to the person. *Journal of Clinical Psychology: In Session, 67*(2), 127–132. doi: 10.1002/jclp.20764

OPD Task Force. (Ed.) (2001). *OPD Operationalized Psychodynamic Diagnostics: Foundations and practical handbook.* Bern, Switzerland: Hogrefe & Huber. (In German: Arbeitskreis OPD. (Ed.). (2006). *Operationalisierte Psychodynamische Diagnostik OPD 2: Das Manual für Diagnostik und Therapieplanung.* Bern, Switzerland: Huber)

Perepletchikova, F., Treat, T. A. & Kazdin, A. E. (2007). Treatment integrity in psychotherapy research: Analysis of the studies and examination of the associated factors. *Journal of Consulting and Clinical Psychology, 75, pp. 829–841.* doi:10.1037/0022-006X.75.6.829

Perls, F. S., Hefferline, R. F. & Goodman, P. (1951). *Gestalt Therapy: Excitement and growth in the human personality.* New York: Julian Press.

Rochet-Capellan, A. & Fuchs, S. (2014). Take a breath and take the turn: How breathing meets turns in spontaneous dialogue. Retrieved from rstb.royalsocietypublishing.org

Rosenberg, J. L., Rand, M. L. & Asay, D. (1996). *Körper, Selbst und Seele: Ein Weg zur Integration* [Body, self, and mind: A way to integration]. Paderborn, Germany: Junfermann.

Roth, G. (1994). *Das Gehirn und seine Wirklichkeit: Kognitive Neurobiologie und ihre philosophischen Konsequenzen* [The brain and its reality: Cognitive neurobiology and its philosophical consequences]. Frankfurt, Germany: Suhrkamp.

Sternberg, S. (1975). Memory scanning: New findings and current controversies. *Quarterly Journal of Experimental Psychology* 27, 1–32. doi: dx.doi.org/10.1080/14640747508400459

Tschuschke, V., Crameri, A., Koehler, M., Berglar, J., Muth, K., Staczan, P., von Wyl, A., Schulthess, P. & Koemeda-Lutz, M. (2015) The role of therapists' treatment adherence, professional experience, therapeutic alliance, and clients' severity of psychological problems Prediction of treatment outcome in eight different psychotherapy approaches. Preliminary results of a naturalistic study. *Psychotherapy Research*, (25) 4, 2015, 420–434

Tschuschke, V., Koemeda-Lutz, M., & Schlegel, M. (2014). *Ratingmanual für psychotherapeutische Konzepttreue*: Praxisstudie ambulante Psychotherapie Schweiz (PAP-S) der Institute der Schweizer Charta für Psychotherapie [Rating manual for psychotherapeutic treatment adherence: Practice Outpatient Psychotherapy Study Switzerland (PAP-S) of the Institute of the Swiss Charta of Psychotherapy].

von Wyl, A., Crameri, A., Koemeda-Lutz, M., Tschuschke, V., & Schulthess, P. (2013). Praxisstudie ambulante Psychotherapie Schweiz (PAP-S): Studiendesign und Machbarkeit [Practice Outpatient Psychotherapy Study Switzerland (PAPS): Study design and feasibility]. *Psychotherapie-Wissenschaft, 1*, 6–22.

About the Authors

Margit Koemeda-Lutz: PhD, psychologist, psychotherapist and faculty member of the IIBA; coordinating trainer for the SGBAT (Swiss Society for Bioenergetic Analysis and Therapy). Co-founding member of the PAP-S research group.

Margit Koemeda-Lutz
E-mail: koemeda@bluewin.ch

Aureliano Crameri, MSc, is a PhD candidate, research associate, psychologist, quality manager, and academic instructor of research methodology at Zurich University for Applied Sciences.

Aureliano Crameri
E-mail: aureliano.crameri@zhaw.ch

Peter Schulthess, MSc, is an instructional therapist and psychotherapist; education leader at the Institute for Integrative Gestalt Therapy Switzerland; and president of the Swiss Charta for Psychotherapy

Peter Schulthess
E-mail: praesidium@psychotherapiecharta.ch

Agnes von Wyl, PhD, is a professor, psychologist; lecturer; and head of the Research Unit for Psychotherapy and Mental Health at Zurich University for Applied Sciences.

Agnes von Wyl
E-mail: vonw@zhaw.ch

Volker Tschuschke, PhD, is a professor, professor emeritus, psychologist, psychoanalyst, formerly head of the department of Medical Psychology at the University Hospital of Cologne, Germany; currently head of the graduate program in psychology at the Sigmund Freud Private University, Berlin.

Volker Tschuschke
E-mail:volker.tschuschke@sfu-berlin.de

Body Resonance and the Voice[1]

Vita Heinrich-Clauer

Abstracts

English

This article focuses on bioenergetic principles and the link between emotions and the voice, discussing various approaches to vocal expression in the psychotherapeutic process. There is an examination of the idiosyncrasies of bioenergetic work with the voice in contrast to therapeutic approaches that work solely with the body. There is an important distinction for practical bioenergetic work between liberating vocal discharge on the one hand and the build-up of tone, boundaries and self-efficacy on the other hand (cf. Shapiro, 2006, 2008, 2009).

Key words: bioenergetic vocal expression, vocal discharge, charging-containing, tonicity.

German

Dieser Beitrag zielt auf bioenergetische Prinzipien in Bezug auf die Verknüpfung von Emotion und Stimme. Verschiedene Ansätze zum stimmlichen Ausdruck im psychotherapeutischen Prozess werden diskutiert, wobei die Besonderheiten bioenergetischer Arbeit mit der Stimme im Unterschied zu reinen körperthe-

1 Lecture delivered March 7th, 2014 in Papenburg, Germany at NIBA's student information day.

rapeutischen Ansätzen herausgestellt werden. Es gibt eine wichtige Unterscheidung in der praktischen bioenergetischen Arbeit: einerseits kann eine befreiende stimmliche Entladung (discharge) und andererseits eine tonisierende, die Grenzen und Selbstwirksamkeit fördernde Vorgehensweise bewirkt werden (charging-containing, vgl. Shapiro, 2006, 2008, 2009).

French

Cet article met l'accent sur les principes d'analyse bioénergétique et le lien existant entre émotion et voix en analysant diverses approches à l'expression vocale à l'intérieur du processus thérapeutique. On y examine les idiosyncrasies propres au travail d'analyse bioénergétique avec la voix en opposition aux approches thérapeutiques travaillant uniquement avec le corps. Il existe une différence importante en matière de travail pratique en analyse bioénergétique entre la décharge vocale d'une part et le développement du ton, des frontières et de l'efficacité, d'autre part. (cf. Shapiro, 2006, 2008. 2009).

Spanish

Este artículo se centra en los principios bioenergéticos y la relación entre las emociones y la voz, y trata de diversos enfoques acerca de la expresión vocal en el proceso psicoterapéutico. También presenta una evaluación de la idiosincrasia del trabajo bioenergético con la voz, en contraste con los enfoques terapéuticos que se centran únicamente en el cuerpo. Hay un distinción importante para el trabajo bioenergético práctico entre por una parte, liberar la descarga vocal, y la acumulación de tono, límites y la autoeficacia por la otra (cf. Shapiro, 2006, 2008, 2009).

Portuguese

Este artigo focaliza princípios bioenergéticos e a conexão entre as emoções e a voz, discutindo várias abordagens da expressão vocal no processo psicoterapêutico. Avalia, ainda, as idiossincrasias do trabalho bioenergético com a voz, em contraste com abordagens terapêuticas que trabalham somente o corpo. Mostra, também, que há uma importante distinção, para a prática do trabalho bioenergético, entre a liberação de uma descarga vocal, de um lado e a construção do tom, limites e auto-eficácia de outro (cf Shapiro, 2006, 2008, 2009).

1. Introduction

An embodied voice transmits and reveals something about the truth of our own person. The sound of our voice offers a more genuine form of self-expression than our speech, which is controlled by the left hemisphere of our brain. Free vocal expression can help release pent up emotions, animate our bodies and touch the people around us. The resonant voice reflects, even more than the speaking voice, something about our current internal state and our current mood, as well as about deeper levels of our selves (cf. Alavi Kia in, 2001, 2009). The sound of the voice lets us differentiate one emotion from another based on tempo, articulation and pitch, as well as the corresponding length of the intonation of vowels and consonants.

> "The voice is so closely linked to your personality that [...] a patient's neurosis can even be diagnosed from a voice analysis" (Lowen, 1979, p. 236).

And:

> "A balanced voice consists of a harmonious combination of chest and head tones. An unbalanced voice inevitably points to a personality problem" (ibid., p. 238).

Wilhelm Reich and *Alexander Lowen* have – in contrast to *Sigmund Freud* – convincingly taught the essential importance of working with breath and the voice to facilitate opening to deeper emotions and to more vibrant vitality. *Reich* was the first to discover that physical work with a client's breath can open up a special gateway to memories and emotions. In doing so, he distanced himself from the abstinent, verbal, psychoanalytic technique of Freud.

Every bioenergetic analyst is familiar with working with the breath, with energy flow and with vocal expression, since it is one of the basic pillars of our method – in addition to work on grounding. Bioenergetic Analysis has taught us to "release the sound." Lowen primarily speaks of a "liberation" of sound. However, it is not easy to express oneself in a spontaneous way that comes from your true self! The energetic "door opener" that is the voice deserves more attention in bioenergetic therapy. Simply encouraging clients to just let the voice "come" is not enough since frequently it doesn't come at all. Or it may emerge as a vegetative expression (sometimes referred to as body memory) without reference to a clear feeling and without a relationship context.

Lowen's first session with Reich: "vegetative screaming from bioenergetic techniques without reference to emotions"
As I was lying on the bed, nothing happened at first. Reich: "Lowen, you're not breathing at all" (my chest remained motionless while breathing). After some time breathing again while lying down "Reich commanded: 'Lowen, let your head fall back and open up your eyes wide!' I did so, and […] had to suddenly scream out loud" (Lowen, 1979, p. 10f.).

> "Oddly enough, the scream did not disturb me. I had no emotional relationship to it." After repeating the procedure: "The scream 'came' once again. I don't want to say that *I* was screaming because I wasn't under the impression that I was doing it. The scream just 'happened' to me. Once again, I had actually nothing to do with it at all" (ibid., p. 11).

> "When the session was over and I had left Reich, I had the feeling that not everything was as alright with me as I had thought. There were 'things' – images, emotions – in my personality that were hidden from my conscious mind, and then I realized that they had to come out" (ibid.).

After a year of therapy with Reich: "sobbing triggered by connotative words relating to emotions"

> "After a year of therapy, I was at an impasse. Since we saw no way out, Reich suggested I discontinue the therapy. 'Lowen,' he said,' you're simply unable to give in to your feelings. Don't you think you should stop?' His words were a condemnation. Quitting would have meant the end of my dreams. I broke down and cried. It was the first time since childhood that I was sobbing. I could no longer hide my feelings. I told Reich what I wanted from him and he listened attentively. I still do not know whether Reich wanted to actually quit the therapy or whether his proposal was only a maneuver to break my internal barrier. In any case, at the time I was under the impression that he was serious. And the result was that the therapy took effect again" (ibid., p. 14).

> "After the crying fit and the expression of my feelings towards Reich, my breathing became lighter and freer, my sexual responsiveness deeper and more complete" (ibid.).

2. Various Approaches to Working with the Voice in Body Oriented Psychotherapy

The focus on the breath and the vocal expression of emotions is an important aspect of many body psychotherapies – unfortunately not of every psychotherapy! There are important differences in working with the voice in bioenergetic analysis and in pure body therapies, as well as between bioenergetics and other emotion centered body psychotherapies. Below is an overview of the most well-known methods with a focus on the voice.

Body therapy (practical-functional)

- Vocal and theatrical training (Kristin Linklater, Alavia Kia)
- Laughter Yoga, bipolar breathwork, respiratory therapy (Ilse Middendorf)
- Martial arts (Wen Do, Karate, Kung Fu, etc.)

Body psychotherapy (biographical, centered on emotion)

- Primal therapy (primal scream, Janov)
- Greek mourning ceremonies (J. Canacakis)
- Other body oriented psychotherapies: Biosynthesis, Core Energetics, Biodynamics, Psychodrama, Gestalt, Analytic Body Psychotherapy, Sensory-motor Psychotherapy
- Bioenergetic Analysis (Lowen, Bob Lewis, Ben Shapiro)

A second glance reveals the fundamental differences in these approaches, particularly from the standpoint of a cognitive-verbal oriented *"top-down"* vs. energetic-somatic *"bottom-up"* processes. Furthermore, we see how difficult it is to integrate a kind of "doing the sound" with emotional comprehension and self-regulation. And not many approaches focus on that.

It is important to look at how the client is invited to learn about his/her voice. Do we rely on verbal interventions only or do we trust the body in a more basic sense? We may start by verbally exploring memories regarding the voice or "landscapes of dealing with vocalizations in the family." It is useful to explore this biographical information within the framework of resistance analysis and not to rush into the bioenergetic mode of "making a sound." One might ask, "Who was allowed in your family to be loud? When? Where? Were sounds of pain permitted? Or was the message, 'Boys don't cry!'"? Were joyful sounds heard in the family?" We can verbally explore in the here and now with the question: "What sound might belong to this sensation or memory?" This is often answered with, "to make sounds and noise is too embarrassing to me, especially on command." This vocal self-inquiry may initially be met with a considerable shame barrier (cf. Moser, 2013, p. 452f.).

If this therapeutic approach is formulated in the subjunctive – on the left-hemispheric level – clients are asked to reflect on and, at most, produce a sound. We, too, are aware of this response from our clients in bioenergetic therapy. Also, the response often not only reveals the shame the client feels, but also their clear refusal to *have to* do something that is just not that easy to do.

In bioenergetic analysis we focus on biographical and on relational aspects in the here and now of the therapeutic encounter as well as on energetic processes (catharsis vs. containment). We can rely on a variety of basic bioenergetic interventions to foster vocal expression in order to work with emotional regulation. In chapter 5 and 6 energetically based interventions will be addressed.

3. On the Neurophysiology of the Voice and Relationship: Porges' Polyvagal Theory

Charles Darwin believed that both language and music emerged from a common musical "proto-language" used to communicate emotions, territorial behavior and during courtship (cf. Darwin, 2000). The voice touches the other and enables communication without words. The resonance of the social environment is solicited via timbre, melody and volume (social overture, seeking an echo). In psychotherapy, the rhythm and amplitude of the therapist's own breathing is critical in detecting the body and feelings of the client. The difference between pure body therapies, such as massage, physiotherapy, osteopathy, etc. and bioenergetic analysis is found when one understands that in bioenergetic analysis the relationship-creating gestures or bodily contact tied to relationship images stimulates clients reactions via the ventral vagus.

Calming yourself and calming the other person in threatening situations is another special feature of the voice.

Facial Expression and Vocalization

Porges' Polyvagal Theory (2010) has given us the tripartite structure of the autonomic nervous system (ANS): in addition to the sympathetic fight-flight reaction, the vagus is also divided into a dorsal vagal complex (= DVC) that originates in the dorsal brainstem and a ventral vagal complex (= VVC) that originates in a ventral originating core. The DVC is regarded as a relic of an immobilization system from the reptilian era. During conditions of rest, it stimulates regular digestive processes. Existential threatening situations, however, lead to a massive stimulation of the DVC with immobilizing and death feigning/dissociative reactions (Porges, 2010, p. 165). The VVC facilitates experiencing and expressing primary emotions and social communication. There is a coupling for regulating gaze and attention, facial expressions, prosody and the ability to listen (ibid., p. 75f; cf. also Clauer, 2013, p. 283–285).

The *ventral vagus complex* (*VVC*), which comprises the NA (ventral nucleus ambigus) and the nuclei of the trigeminal and facial nerves, is clearly related to expression and the experience of emotions (ibid., p. 77). The capacity for social engagement depends on how well we can influence our facial and cranial muscles using nerve (corticobulbar) pathways that interconnect the cortex and the brain stem. These muscles make our face capable of showing expression and allow us to communicate meaning through gestures, to influence the sound of our voice, to turn our gaze to specific things and to use our hearing to differentiate human voices from background noise. The neuronal control of facial and cranial muscles influences how people perceive the efforts of others to enter into relationship with them.

A negative affective state (negative primary emotion) would reduce the tone of the entire vagal branch (VVC). It originates in the NA geared to promoting fight or flight behavior. A reduced tone (triggered by an external or internal threatening situation) leads to *reduced social engagement*:

- The eyelids droop.
- The voice loses its ability to modulate, gets flat.
- Positive facial expressions are rare.
- The sound of human voices is perceived indistinctly.
- Sensitivity of the efforts by others to establish social contact decreases.

A higher VVC tone (seen in secure situations) allows one to:

- express oneself with an appealing vocal tone and speech rhythm,
- show a friendly facial expression,
- influence middle ear muscles in such a way that human voices can be clearly distinguished from background noise,
- make eye contact, and
- to have a *reduction of social distance* (cf. ibid., p. 35f.).

In socially safe situations, the *"prosocial" VVC,* with its so-called vagal brake, therefore inhibits the mobilizing fight or flight readiness of the sympathetic nervous system and the immobilizing emergency reactions of the DVC. The concept of *neuroception* describes a person's vigilant scanning of the environment for hazards and existential threats.

> "The neuroception of familiar people as well as people with a confidence-inspiring and empathetic sounding voice and a corresponding facial expression leads to a social interaction that promotes a sense of security" (ibid., p. 90).

Porges provides evidence of hemispheric differences and a vagal lateralization, according to which a relationship exists between the function of the right hemisphere and primary emotions.

> "The primary chronotropic output of the heart comes from the right NA (ventral nucleus ambigus) via the right cardiac vagus nerve. The special visceral efferent fibers that allow behaviors through which emotions are defined (facial expression and vocalization) also have a right hemispheric tendency and are neuroanatomically connected to the general visceral efferent fibers emanating from the NA that regulate the bronchial tubes and the heart – organs assumed to be sensitive to emotions and stress" (ibid., p. 76).

These neurophysiological studies do not make a distinction between the sensation of a negative affective state and their expression. In this case, it would be interesting to see whether differences could be observed in a person's physiological responses at the ANS level, when there is a way to express emotions such as anger, sadness and joy.

Case Vignette 1

Manual interventions in a situation where one has no opportunity to make a sound that reflects pain and is in an insecure therapeutic relationship

A currently clearly depressed client reports her dentist's intensive work on resetting her jaw. It was enormously strenuous for her to keep her mouth open for the time required, since she has a history of abuse, a long-standing anxiety disorder and social phobia. Because of the massive neck and jaw tension that resulted from her dental treatment, the dentist suggested that she see a physiotherapist for chiropractic and manual therapy. The client says that the well-intentioned physiotherapist's manual manipulation was even worse than her dental treatment, since she experienced tremendous pain and could not express it. She says that her relationship with her dentist was good but that of her physical therapist lacked warmth and was technically oriented, as he showed no personal feedback whatsoever.

After her session with me she told her physiotherapist at her next appointment that her psychotherapist had told her that moaning or crying in pain would reduce the pain. The physical therapist subsequently closed the windows and was personally attentive to her for the first time. That helped her to have a reduction of pain during the following treatment.

This regulation of the relationship can be understood both in the sense of Porges' SES and in a bio-energetic sense. The difference between body therapies like massage, physiotherapy, etc. and in bioenergetic analysis (and other body psychotherapies that work with relationships) is that relationship-creating gestures or bodily contact associated with relational images stimulates other reactions via the vagus than the mere mechanical contact of a stranger (cf. section 3).

4. General Bioenergetic Aspects: Movement – Grounding – Breathing – Emotionality – Motility – Stress – Vocal Expression

Our breathing is organized by reflexes. It is a pulsation: contraction – expansion. The breath wave normally flows from our mouth to the genitals.

As long as we breathe, we live. We cannot commit suicide simply by holding our breath. As long as we breathe, we feel. Deep breathing improves the motility of our muscles as well as improving the natural vibration of our body, which is the prerequisite for vocal expression. We can inhale "to the fullest" or restrict our breathing and our vital contact with the environment by placing it (breathing) on the "back burner." Breathing fully brings pleasure and joie de vivre (although excess oxygen creates an increased drive and a sense of urgency or anxiety). Shallow breathing results in lack of oxygen and limits our vitality and emotion in such a way that we produce little vibrant impulse and correspondingly receive little feedback (classic depressive pattern). The emotional expression while making sounds provides us with stimulation via vibration and self-massage, while reducing rigidity, stiffness, silence, depression and introjects.

Breathing is the central key to perceiving emotions and expressing these with the voice – or to controlling emotions by holding our breath and taking shallow breaths.

Core feelings such as sadness, anger, fear, disgust, desire and joy are kept in check by regulating breathing. "When an emotion is blocked it cannot be expressed well vocally" (Lowen, 1979, p. 237).

The blockage involves all the contractile muscles of the upper body (mouth and jaw muscles, tongue, neck, intercostal muscles, etc.) as well as the pelvic muscles.

The respiratory muscles: diaphragm, intercostal muscles, pelvic floor muscles, shoulder girdle and neck also contract when breathing is restricted.

There is less expansion in the diaphragm between the lowest lumbar vertebrae, the sternum and the lower rib cage.

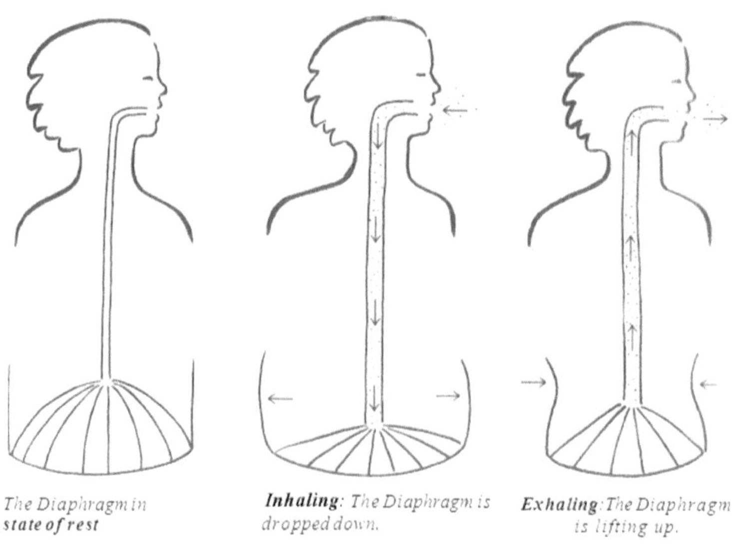

Figure 1. Diaphragmatic movement while breathing

When inhaling, the diaphragm actively moves downward, which creates a vacuum that is followed by the passive inhalation of air through the airways.

Inhalation actively sucks in air and takes in oxygen, which enriches the blood. This offers an intensive "internal contact" with the environment via the surface of the respiratory organs. On the muscular level, the following occurs:

- ➢ the diaphragm drops and expands the chest area downwards,
- ➢ the ribs open up like blinds,
- ➢ the lumbar spine becomes erect (slight hollow back),
- ➢ the pelvis pulls itself slightly back,
- ➢ the spine makes a wave motion,
- ➢ the upper body expands,
- ➢ the changed muscle tone and the erect position show tonicity.

Inhalation and the tension in the diaphragm *massage the abdominal organs (rhythm of the intestine, bladder, sexual organs, sexuality!).* Deep breathing involves all the stabilizing core muscles, including the pelvic floor (*grounding and sexuality!*).

Exhalation releases air to the environment again (with the waste product carbon dioxide). Discharging air is a relief and a "burden" on the environment. On the muscular level, the following occurs:

- ➢ the diaphragm lifts,
- ➢ the intercostal and stomach muscles contract,
- ➢ the pelvis tilts forward and down,
- ➢ the lumbar spine expands backwards and down,
- ➢ the upper body loses volume,
- ➢ the decreased muscle tone indicates flexibility (possibly emptiness).

When *exhaling*, the diaphragm moves back up to the fifth/sixth rib, the chest expands, the intercostal muscles stretch. In doing so, the *heart* is also massaged on the exhalation *(sighing, toning, lamenting, liberation from old pain and alleviation of the heart).*

Breathing is done by the muscles in the shoulder girdle and neck, which lift the clavicles (*opening the esophagus: anxiety crying, sucking in air, taking for yourself*).

The following poem by Erich Fried touchingly describes the relationship between exhalation and emotionality:

Revocation
Being able to exhale your unhappiness
Exhale deeply
so that you can inhale again
And maybe being able to articulate your unhappiness
in words
in real words

that are coherent and make sense
that you can still understand yourself
and that perhaps even someone else understands too
or could understand
And being able to cry
That would almost be happiness again

Lowen speaks about "freeing the path of communication from the heart to the world" when we work with segments in the body. There are three segments of the body that can develop rings of tension from chronic holding, which narrow the channel and prevent the full expression of feelings. These tension rings are not anatomical but functional units.

1. The outermost segment ring forms around the mouth. A firm or closed mouth can block any communication of feelings. Compressed lips and a locked jaw prevent sounds from making their way out into the open (Lowen, 1979, p. 241).
2. The second segment ring of tension is formed at the junction of the head and neck. It represents the transition from voluntary to involuntary control. The throat and mouth lie in front of this area; the esophagus and trachea are behind it. Things you don't want to swallow are controlled here. In this segment is an unconscious defense mechanism against the expression of unacceptable feelings. The tension affects breathing and contributes to feelings of anxiety (ibid., p. 241f.).

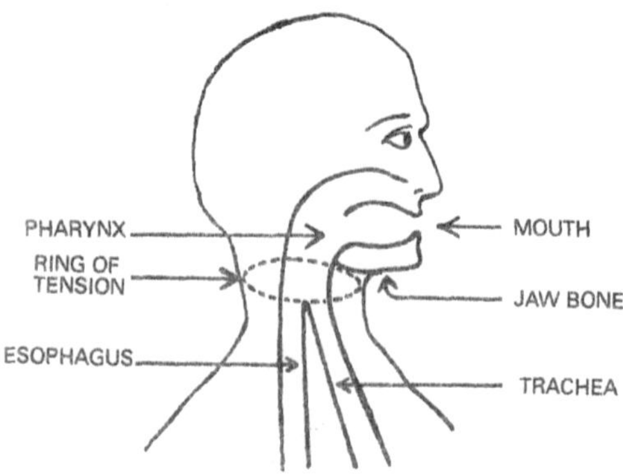

Figure 2. Ring of tension at the junction of the head and neck

3. The third segment ring is seen in the connection of the neck and thorax: the front, middle and rear scalene (rib holding) muscles are involved. This ring of tension guards the opening of the rib cage and thus the heart. When these muscles are chronically contracted, they arch up and make the upper ribs immobile which constricts the opening to the chest. Because this obstructs natural respiratory movements, voice production is impaired. This applies particularly to the chest register (ibid., p. 244f.).

According to Lowen, a lack of vibrations indicates stress and holding back either in the body or in the voice.

> "A person who does not vibrate is under stress or holding back when it comes to his/her body and his/her voice. In the voice, a lack of vibration leads to a loss of resonance" (ibid., p. 237).

Stress = Holding back = Loss of Vibration = Flatness/Lack of emotions and feelings.

Moreover, shallow breathing, lack of vibration and reduced motility *weaken* our immune system, while deep breathing, vocal expression, laughter and singing *positively stimulate* our immune system on the hormonal level. In some clinics, especially in pediatrics, doctors specifically employ "laughter therapy" (e.g. with hospital clowns) in order to take away patients fear of surgery. Laughing patients require fewer painkillers (cf. Spiecker-Henke, 2013; Kreutz, 2014).

In some fifth to sixth grade math classes, screaming is encouraged to promote concentration. According to their math teacher this is enhancing the children's concentration if it's done every 20 minutes!

5. Special Features of Bioenergetic Work with Emotions and the Voice: Motoric and Vocal Expression and Hands-on Techniques

Lowen recognizes the need to not only work on emotional blockages but also specifically on the voice in order to loosen tension. In doing so, the focus is more on spontaneous sounds and on the *liberation of repressed emotions*, via the release of tension in the muscles involved.

The following techniques are used to coordinate motoric and vocal expression:

1. Lying down, kicking on a mattress with your legs, while shouting "Why?", "No!" or "Leave me alone!"
2. Hitting foam cubes with a tennis racket, shouting "Hah" or "No".
3. Using a breathing stool, or Pezzi ball to alleviate the pain and sadness of the heart with an "Ah" sound in an elongated exhalation.

Lowen describes various hands-on techniques to open up vocal blockages and release repressed emotions (Lowen, 1979, p. 240f.):

1. Putting continuous pressure (a John Pierrakos technique) on the *scalene muscles and the sternocleidomastoid muscle*. While doing so, the client is encouraged to emit a constant, high-pitched tone. If no scream comes, says Lowen, he stops pressing and accepts the resistance.
2. Pressing on the masseter muscle, while the client is lying down and kicking the bed with a loud protesting sound. The opening of the jaw, which he called the "gate of the personality," is regarded as the key to all other blocking mechanisms in the body.

> "Although you can do a good job inducing screams with this method, it still does not reduce all the tension that has formed around the mouth and throat that inhibits generating tones. When a person's voice is free, it comes from the heart" (ibid., p. 241).

It is important not to assume that a deliberately produced sound (or even the bioenergetic "disposition" of moaning and screaming) too soon is a release. It may be that it represents a physical release of tension only, which is an important first step (see the explanation and Lowen's first session with Reich earlier in this article).

> "If an expression of feeling confirms the self, then the mind and body must always interact. That's why crying or even screaming has no therapeutic effect as long as we don't know why we're crying and aren't able to talk about it" (cf. Lowen, 1993, p. 74).

Therapists are encouraged to stay attentive and listen to the sounds that reach us to determine whether or not this sound is associated with a core emotion or an authentic non-verbal statement about the self.

In order to spontaneously develop a sound or a spontaneous tone a client may need:

- ➢ bioenergetic techniques
- ➢ somatic resonance of the therapist
- ➢ verbal support and comprehension
- ➢ encouragement to express feelings and sounds

If we are experiencing an emotionality, a somatic resonance – specifically in certain areas of the body – and *not just an intense loud noise*, then we (as therapists) feel emotionally connected to the client. We work with our clients to find an authentic sound with the contact or by using hands-on techniques on the neck, jaw, or even with cooperation (joint toning with the client). In case of any inhibitions, feelings of being stuck or artificial statements about the self, we try to change the client's expression by requesting the client repeat their sentence again with a relaxed jaw to amplify this without stress in the throat. We may try vocal accompaniment to facilitate a flowing, harmonious and touchingly spontaneous expression.

6. Differentiation of Bioenergetic Concepts and Methodology when Working with Vocal Expression

Discharging Pain, Fear, Anger – Release – Surrender

The voice can be used to provide relief and release in the therapeutic process.

Release takes place in the exhalation, which can free pent up emotions and release the muscle groups involved. Vocal expression with emotional content (pain, fear, anger) generates vibrations and works via the self-massage from the inside, like a sensory confirmation, a *surrender to your own body* (cf. Lowen, 1993).

> "However, the goal of therapy is not only to liberate the voice, but to coordinate free vocal expression with the corresponding free physical expression through movement" (cf. ibid., p. 138).

Coordinating free vocal expression with free physical expression can be seen as follows:

1. The voice sometimes lets me discover my *mood* (self-perception on the auditory and proprioceptive level) and improve my mood. It can offer self-assurance that I am alive, I breathe, I make sound, I am there. I use it to touch myself and others.

2. The voice can help me develop harmony with myself (e.g. sighing and plaintive sounds), loosen rigidity and let go of the abdomen and pelvis, experience the resonance of my own body and experience soft feelings. Or I can give room to my rage, by spitting it out instead of swallowing it, or by screaming. A feeling of relief and joy is often the result.
3. The voice and the opening of the throat, (the "pipes") dissolves pain. This is because pain is reduced with crying, which can relax the muscles).

Case Vignette 2:[2] Exhalation and Processing Pain

This case study helps clarify the relationship of breathing, vocalization and processing pain based on an excerpt from the 39th therapy session with a 37-year-old man, Mr. F. The client was suffering from anxiety, panic attacks, insomnia and stomach problems. He showed a preference for sadomasochistic practices.

As I firmly massaged his cranial base muscles, he did not utter a sound. After I paused and jokingly told him I don't intend to break my thumb in today's session, he replied: "That's just it! If I don't make a sound, that increases the pain and the pleasure!"

This statement made a lot of sense, since the client said he was into S&M techniques! I replied, "Oh Gosh, I totally forgot about that." I was naive, or put positively, I was uninformed regarding S&M techniques. But then I explained that toning and release of (old) pain and anxiety was, among other things, a therapeutic goal of bioenergetic analysis and that all body cells can expand and relax when exhaling. Pain can be reduced when we make a sound.

The client listened attentively to this and said, "Ok, I'll try to make a sound."

I told him that his sexual practices/preferences might change when he changes his emotional (pain) processing mode.

He then replied: "Yes, if it happens as you say, I'll just accept it as such. I'll take that chance."

That was what happened: Mr. F. separated from his wife (his S&M companion), fell in love with a less obsessive young woman, switched to "normal" sexual positions and had a child. In addition, he lost his phobia of highway driving and his hypochondriacal fear of a heart attack.

---

2 This case has been described in more detail in another therapy sequence published by Clauer and Heinrich 1999. For this publication, the client's consent was given so that the current description of the case does not breach the rules of patient confidentiality.

Case Vignette 3: Rage and Fear

A colleague in training discussed her insomnia in an encounter group. Afraid of her first consulting sessions, she was not able to sleep for two nights and was plagued by doubts about her skills. She was not able to sleep in the seminar house. A first diagnosis of her posture while standing revealed raised, tense shoulders and an anxious expression in her eyes. She reported having "frozen shoulder" syndrome. The body-oriented constellation of her relevant biographical scenario revealed the image of her three older brothers who she experienced as a burden on her shoulders and pressed her down. In the past, they would frighten her with their pranks and torture her. She remembers how she had, when she was four years old, once crossed the courtyard in the dark of night to go the outhouse and how her brothers turned off the light as she sat there alone.

She screamed in terror. Her parents did not notice their wicked game in the outhouse or her distress. Today, as an adult, she is not able to scream and feels imprisoned in her body whenever she is confronted by excessive demands. While working on this scenario, she gradually summed up enough courage to raise her voice and shout "Stop it" at a gradually increased pitch until finally emitting a spectacular cry that filled the entire room! As a result, her shoulder muscles relaxed; her frightened eyes relaxed as well. She slept well in the seminar house that night.

At home, she now regularly practices screaming in her car on the way to her counseling work and reports that she is able to sleep again.

Special Exercises that Relax the Voice and Prepare for "Discharge"

Anger/Protest:
Lying on the bed rhythmically kicking and/or crying "Why?" (sound sustained as long as possible). The "Why?" is raised to a scream while quickly and intensely kicking. Shouting while car driving (cf. Lowen, 1993, p. 138).

Jaw/Tongue:
Yawning, making grimaces with the jaw and lips, sticking the tongue out left and right, panting like a thirsty little dog.

Eyes/Head/Neck:
Rolling the head on the floor, receiving a neck massage and toning.

Laughing:
Arching the head backwards, laughing "Ha, ha, ha ..." (cf. Shapiro, 2008, p. 79).

Fear:
Imagining something on the ceiling that triggers fear. Then inhaling with the sounds of fear, exaggerate this sound, then lower the head, exhale, and let go (while standing). Next, do the same exercise as the Cow/Cat position in Yoga. (get on the floor, on hands and knees, alternating concave and convex rounding of the back).

Craziness:
Sticking the tongue out to the left and right, make silly laughter, "Meeting of village idiots" (ibid., p. 69).

Sounds fall out:
Lying down, lift the pelvis and drop it to the floor and let a sound fall out while exhaling; in the same position, lift your chest off the ground and drop it to the floor with your upper back, letting a sound fall out while exhaling.

Charging, Toning, Building Boundaries and Containment, Self-Efficacy

Bioenergetic analysis understands resilience and vocal expressiveness as a physical concept. These depend not only on the perception of one's muscular strength but substantially on the capacity to breathe deeply and to have vocal expression (cf. Heinrich-Clauer, 2014; also Spiecker-Henke, 2013; Kreutz, 2014). The voice may be used to tonify and establish boundaries, that is, to invigorate in the sense of resilience and expressiveness. In this regard, the work of Ben Shapiro in particular represent a complement to and creative extension of the basic bioenergetic techniques since these direct one's focus on charging, containing and boundary techniques (cf. Shapiro, 2006, 2008, 2009).

Deep *inhalation* expands the upper body and straightens the thoracic spine. The pelvis pulls back slightly. This allows one to define his/her personal space in relation to the other and to have a contact boundary. The emphasized short inhalation creates the moment of tension! *The altered muscle tone and the erect posture demonstrate vigor.*

If one takes advantage of this charge to make an increasingly powerfully held sound, instead of letting go when exhaling (as in sighing or moaning), the defining effect is reinforced and this is a charge in the body at the same time (toning).

- ➢ Toning is used to strengthen the body's boundaries, to build up structure and delineate it from the social environment. This allows one to distinguish between me and you.
- ➢ Increased self-efficacy through controlled tones: by making oneself noticeable through held and controlled breath, one also appears self-effective in relation to the social world.

Special Exercises to Build up Boundaries and for Containment (Charge)

Boundary, voice:
Partner exercises: standing across from one another, saying: "No – Yes"; "I have the final say!"; "Do it the way I want!"

Boundary, mouth/lips:
Making sharp loud sounds like, "ssssh," and "pphaa!"

Boundary, diaphragm:
Crying "Hah!" while standing across from a partner, keeping the partner away with forcefully emitted sounds.

Boundary, neck:
Start in the hanging over position against the wall or against the hip of a partner. While pressure is exerted by the upper back, shoulder girdle and neck exhale, raise your voice, making it louder – up to the climax of control! (Don't wait until the sound decreases.)

Boundary, arms:
Wringing a towel or flex rod, holding your voice as long as you can and maintain the tension in your hands/arms (cf. Shapiro, 2006, p. 161).

Boundary, pelvis:
Taking the semi-position on the breathing stool, moving the jaw out, pushing the pelvis forward while exhaling (or: therapist exerts counter-pressure with her hands).

Containment:
Lying on your stomach, tensing all back and leg muscles, lifting your head, raise your voice, scream "I caaaaaannnn!" – stopping at the peak of your voice/muscle control.

7. Conclusion

The energetic "door opener" that is the voice deserves more attention in bioenergetic therapy. We can rely on a variety of basic bioenergetic interventions to foster vocal expression in order to work with emotional regulation. The emotional expression while making sounds provides us with stimulation via vibration and self-massage while reducing rigidity, stiffness, silence, depression and introjects. But simply encouraging clients to just let the voice "come" is not enough since frequently it doesn't come at all. It is important not to assume that a deliberately produced sound (or even the bioenergetic "disposition" of moaning and screaming) too soon is a release. There is an important distinction for practical bioenergetic work between liberating vocal discharge on the one hand and the build-up of tone, boundaries and self-efficacy on the other hand. The voice may be used to tonify and establish boundaries, that is, to invigorate in the sense of resilience and expressiveness.

From a bioenergetic point of view, it is worthwhile to note the expressive gestures of celebratory athletes on the sports pages of your newspaper. Cf. *Video (YouTube): All Blacks Haka.* It will become unfortunately clear that our profession hardly provides this kind of an opportunity to open your mouth and raise your fist in victory. A pity, really!

References

Alavi Kia, R.(2001). *Stimme – Spiegel meines Selbst.* Bielefeld: Aurum Publishers.

Alavi Kia, R.(2009). *Die Musik des Körpers. Integratives Stimmtraining.* Bielefeld: Aurum Publishers.

Clauer J. & Heinrich, V. (1999). Körperpsychotherapeutische Ansätze in der Behandlung traumatisierter Patienten. *Psychother. Forum, 7*, p. 75–93.

Clauer, J. (2013). Psychovegetative Regulation, Kooperation, Triade und das Grounding-Konzept der Bioenergetischen Analyse. In M. Thielen (ed.), *Körper – Gruppe – Gesellschaft* (p. 277–286). Gießen: Psychosozial- Publishers.

Darwin, C. (2000). *Der Ausdruck der Gemütsbewegungen bei dem Menschen und den Tieren.* Frankfurt/M.: Eichborn Publishers.

Heinrich, V. (1997). Körperliche Phänomene der Gegenübertragung. Therapeuten als Resonanzkörper. *Forum Bioenergetische Analyse*, p. 32–41.

Heinrich-Clauer, V. (ed.). (2008). *Handbuch Bioenergetische Analyse.* Gießen: Psychosozial Publishers.

Heinrich-Clauer, V. (2009). Die Rolle der Therapeutin in der Bioenergetischen Analyse. Resonanz, Kooperation, Begreifen. In P. Geißler & V. Heinrich-Clauer (ed.), *Psychoanalyse & Körper, Nr. 15 [Sonderheft: Bioenergetische Analyse im Dialog], 8*, p. 31–55.

Heinrich-Clauer, V. (2013). Wirkfaktoren der Gruppe aus Sicht der Bioenergetischen Analyse. In

M. Thielen (ed.), *Körper – Gruppe – Gesellschaft* (p. 111–121). Gießen: Psychosozial Publishers.
Heinrich-Clauer, V. (2014). Bioenergetische Selbstfürsorge für Therapeuten – Zwischen Öffnung und Abgrenzung. *Forum Bioenergetische Analyse 2014*, p. 9–33.
Kreutz, G. (2014). *Warum Singen glücklich macht*. Gießen: Psychosozial Publishers.
Linklater, K. (1976). *Freeing the Natural Voice*. New York: Drama Publishers. Dt. (2001): *Die persönliche Stimme entwickeln. Ein ganzheitliches Übungsprogramm zur Befreiung der Stimme* (2nd edition). Munich: Ernst Reinhard.
Lowen, A. (1979). *Bioenergetik. Therapie der Seele durch Arbeit mit dem Körper*. Reinbek: Rowohlt Publishers.
Lowen, A. (1993). *Freude. Die Hingabe an den Körper und das Leben*. Munich: Kösel.
Moser, T. (2013). Auf der Suche nach dem stimmigen Ton. *Deutsches Ärzteblatt PP, 12*(10), p. 452–453.
Porges, St. (2010). *Die Polyvagal-Theorie. Neurophysiologische Grundlagen der Therapie. Emotionen, Bindung, Kommunikation und ihre Entstehung*. Paderborn: Junfermann.
Shapiro, B. (2000). Will Iceberg Sink Titanic? *Bioenergetic Analysis, 11*(1), p. 33–42.
Shapiro, B. (2006). Bioenergetic Boundary Building. *Bioenergetic Analysis, 16*, p. 153–178.
Shapiro, B. (2008). Your Core Energy is Within Your Grasp. *Bioenergetic Analysis, 18*, p. 65–91.
Shapiro, B. (2009). Rekindling Pleasure: Seven Exercises for Opening your Heart, Reaching Out and Touching Gently. *Bioenergetic Analysis, 19*, p. 53–84.
Spiecker-Henke, M. (2013). *Leitlinien der Stimmtherapie*. Stuttgart: Thieme Publishers.

About the Author

Dr. Vita Heinrich-Clauer, Dipl. Psych., former researcher and teacher at the University of Osnabrück in psychological diagnostics, psychosomatic medicine, physical diagnostics, and developmental psychology. Since 1989, psychotherapist in private practice, supervisor, lecturer, writer, international trainer for bioenergetic analysis (IIBA faculty).

Dr. Vita Heinrich-Clauer
Krahnstr. 17
49074 Osnabrück
Germany
E-mail: vita.heinrich-clauer@osnanet.de

Rainer Funk, Neil McLaughlin (Eds.)

Towards a Human Science

The Relevance of Erich Fromm for Today

2015 · 322 Pages · Paperback
ISBN 978-3-8379-2535-7

There is a global rediscovery of the ideas and theories of Erich Fromm underway, leading to this book that reviews Fromm's international reception and provides a critical reappraisal of his work rooted in his own philosophy of science that insists on the time-limited nature of all theoretical systems. Because of Fromm's provocative philosophy of science, this volume is entitled Towards a Human Science and begins with the republication of a 1957 essay called The Humanistic Science of Man. Most of the papers in the book have their origins in presentations given at the first International Erich Fromm Research Conference at the International Psychoanalytic University in Berlin (June 2014).

In addition to documenting Fromm's continuing relevance, Towards a Human Science centrally engages with his theoretical system directly and critically, particularly his theory of social character. The book opens paths for research, theories and insights in neurosciences, evolutionary psychology, sociology, philosophy, religious studies and radical humanist public intellectual work. In doing so, this revisit and reappraisal can help us move beyond some of the limitations of his work and reformulate and build on his insights for the 21st century.

Walltorstr. 10 · 35390 Gießen · Tel. 0641-969978-18 · Fax 0641-969978-19
bestellung@psychosozial-verlag.de · www.psychosozial-verlag.de

www.ingramcontent.com/pod-product-compliance
Ingram Content Group UK Ltd.
Pitfield, Milton Keynes, MK11 3LW, UK
UKHW040025200726
13854UKWH00001B/371

9 783837 925043